The
SYSTEM
BUILDER

By
XUAN NGUYEN

Edited by
NICK NGUYEN

Jeany Lih.

Fourth Edition
X PRESS, Alviso, California
www.worldsystembuilder.com

Copyright © 2011 by X PRESS

All rights reserved.
ISBN 978-1-936914-00-5
Published by X PRESS.
2099 Gold Street, PO Box 2028, Alviso, CA 95002

4th Edition - 2011
3rd Edition - 2007
2nd Edition - 2004
1st Publication - 2002

Designed by Tammy Luong.
Printed and bound in the United States.
To purchase copies of this book,
visit www.worldsystembuilder.com
or The Distribution Center at www.wfg-online.com

CONTENTS

The System Flow

The Prospect List

BMP + BPM

Personal Financial Strategy

MD Club

MD

MD Factory

Recruiting

Building

Meetings and Events

Mission

Team Building

Winning Mindset

DISCLAIMER

This book is intended for internal use only, not for public distribution. No part of this book may be reproduced in any form, except for educational and training purposes within the company.

No statement, illustration, graph, or other representation in the training manual is intended to form a contractual agreement or to modify or to supplement any existing contractual agreement between the company, the author, and the members.

Illustrations in the manual of how recruiting others to join our organization can affect commissions of members are not a representation of past or projected future earnings of the members.

The System Builder is intended as a guide to help an agent through the process of building a sales organization. Only licensed individuals may speak about products and services offered. Sales are made based on the needs, product suitability, and affordability of the clients.

The Personal Financial Strategy is a customized suitability and needs analysis. The analysis is based upon information obtained from sources believed to be reliable and accurate. Members are not required to purchase any product or service of any kind in exchange for becoming or remaining a member.

While many people have experienced successful careers, this book represents individual member experiences. As each individual differs, so are his/her specific results. Work ethic patterns, activity levels, and dedication all play significant roles in determining the outcome that one may achieve and in his/her ability to control his/her destiny on an ongoing basis. This statement is not intended to nor does it represent that any current member's individual results are representative of what all participants achieve when following the information contained in this book.

The author and publisher shall have neither liability nor responsibility to any person or entity with respect to any loss or damage caused, or alleged to have been caused, directly or indirectly, by the information contained in this book. This book is sold with the understanding that the publisher and author are not engaged in rendering legal, accounting, or other professional advice or services.

The views and opinions expressed in "The System Builder" are the views of Xuan Nguyen and do not necessarily reflect the views and opinions of any other person or company.

PREFACE

It may sound strange, but even though I grew up in the business, I never really knew what my parents did, and honestly, I never cared to know.

When I first started going to the meetings, I thought the people in the business were a bunch of weirdos. These people worked on Friday nights and Saturday mornings. They had to be crazy. And at conventions, people who looked like adults danced on chairs, wore the same shirt three days in a row, and shouted like cheerleaders. Weird is an understatement.

So when my parents asked me to help out by taking pictures at the annual convention, I came into the event as a skeptical photographer. But I left a true believer.

What I saw amazed me. I saw doctors, lawyers, and engineers abandon their status and security for a dream and a mission. I saw women, minorities, and immigrants leading the doctors, lawyers, and engineers. I saw equality, empowerment, and a passion for a meaningful cause. I saw a business of people helping people. And I too wanted to lend a helping hand.

When the convention was over, I found myself not wanting it to end. I asked my parents when the next convention would take place. They told me March. I'd have to wait two months!

Then it hit me. People are willing to give up their weekends, spend their hard-earned money, and fly across the country to learn how to be successful in this business. "They need this information badly," I thought, "and they need it all the time, especially new people joining the business everyday."

With that in mind, I proposed that my dad gather all of his knowledge and experience into a book, so that anybody, even the newest person, could shorten their learning curve and start building their business as fast as possible.

My dad thought it was great idea. In fact, he told me that for a long time he had wanted to write a book about how to build a successful business through the system.

Due to space constraints, it was impossible for us to cover every topic of this business. But we tried our best to include the issues most relevant to the entrepreneurs who are out in the field making a difference for families and building their businesses every day.

In this fourth edition, we continue to make the system more clear, readable, and enjoyable for the new and existing team member. We hope this book serves as a useful and inspirational guide to builders everywhere.

In concert with the spirit of the team, the creation of this book was a team effort. Many thanks to everyone in the team and the home office for their contributions and feedback.

Nick Nguyen
Editor

INTRODUCTION

It dawned on me while preparing this 4th edition that it has been ten years since I started this project. Believe me: Writing a book had never been my fondest idea, especially when English is not my native language. Furthermore, writing a book about organizing, building, and systematizing a large number of people is an even more momentous task. The irony of all this is that while I express my ideas about it, our team has yet to fully accomplish our mission. It's like a group of miners digging a tunnel through a mountain and writing an instruction book about it at the same time. This book, like our mission, remains a work in progress.

When the new millennium began, my business suffered a prolonged decline. After countless efforts to fix the problem with little results, we realized that a new approach and a new vision were what we needed to build the future. So in January 2001, at Houston's Reliant Park, we launched The System Flow, a simple solution for building a big business.

We were excited by the discovery of a system that would lead a new person step by step from start to finish in their pursuit to become a successful businessperson. It was a refreshing concept because up until that point all we knew was only how to recruit a person, get them out in the field, and help them with the financial solution. But with The System Flow, we were able to push these people to the next level of building a business that lasts.

In the summer of the following year, we released the first edition of *The System Builder* book. It was an attempt to systematize the whole organization through The System Flow. The early version was based on double-digit recruiting in the base called the Contender program.

2004 came, and a new breakthrough for System Builders materialized. The MD Club system emphasized fast start and duplication. The concept of a MD factory meant building more outlets while solidifying building efforts. Continuing to simplify and unify the new system, the second edition of *The System Builder* described how simple, clear, fast, and doable it is for everyone to build.

Great progress follows. The number of both recruits and production steadily improved. As we experienced our new-found success, our understanding of and confidence in the system grew. The third edition of *The System Builder* was thus launched in 2007 to incorporate all the new discoveries. We also added color to the text to make it more readable.

The system works, and we work the system. During this tremendous run from 2007 until today, we focus more on the system—rather than on promotion—to build our business. We improved our meeting mentality, building from event to event. And we continue to simplify our materials and presentation. It's not good enough to tell people to keep it simple. We have to provide them the tools to do it. Thus, this 4th edition is an overdue update on an ongoing process.

The belief in building people and the confidence to build a new distribution system in the financial industry have never been so strong. As we move forward in building the new industry, we do believe that we can work together, utilizing a powerful system, to duplicate and systematize anyone. With strong discipline and a great desire to win, we will build a solid distribution system that will change the world and provide hope to so many people whose lives we touch.

Xuan Nguyen
System Builder

> *What would you do*
> *if you knew exactly how*
> *to win?*
>
> — XUAN NGUYEN

THE SYSTEM FLOW
The MD Factory

MD TRAINEE	MD CLUB	MD	MD FACTORY

"DO IT RIGHT"

"DO IT WITH PRIDE"

"People Gathering"

FAST START
JOIN - OWN - SHARE

- Start Licensing
- Develop a Prospect List
- Match-Up for Field Recruiting (BMP+BPM)
- Finalize your Personal Financial Strategy

"The Big Push"

RECRUIT 3
QUALIFY FOR MD CLUB

Build 3 MD Club legs:

Level 1: 1 MD Club Leg
Level 2: 2 MD Club Legs
Level 3: 3 MD Club Legs

"The Baseshop Building Machine"

QUALIFY FOR MD

Build a large base with
10, 15 and 20 MD Clubs

"The Hierarchy/Outlets Building Machine"

QUALIFY FOR EXECLUB
3 DIRECT MDs

- Be coached by System Builders to become a big builder
- Build a large team of MDs

For internal use only. Not for use with the public.

A Simple Solution for Building a Big Business

THE
SYSTEM FLOW

*If you want
one year of prosperity,
grow grain.
If you want
ten years of prosperity,
grow trees.
If you want
one hundred years of prosperity,
grow people.*

– CHINESE PROVERB

THE SYSTEM BUILDER

"Don't just sell. Build!"

For a long time starting a business was a lonely and risky endeavor. The rate of failure was so high that only a small number of businesses survived. Even for the ones that succeeded, few were able to grow big or transfer the business to the next generation.

All that changed when Ray Kroc started the new marketing revolution with McDonald's franchising system. What was considered unpredictable became quite predictable. What was considered hard to build now became so easy to duplicate. Ray Kroc made McDonald's business model so simple to operate that anyone could do it. This distribution revolution totally changed the way people do business. Whereas before you needed special skills or lots of luck, now all you need is a workable, predictable system.

Look at the Marines. After basic training, men and women come out walking like a Marine, talking like a Marine, dressing like a Marine, and fighting like a Marine. With a proper training system, the Marines can ensure a predictable outcome. McDonald's has similar beliefs. After finishing Hamburger University training, any franchisee can build, operate and open more franchises.

"You run the system. The system will run your business."

The speed of duplication has spread to almost every industry, from food to furniture to fitness. Except for the financial industry. For decades, the old ways of doing the business have barely changed. Most people in the industry are working for financial companies as employees and captive agents. Some are independent brokers or agency owners. But almost all of them are salespeople. A few have agents working for them, but they have no system, they are small, and they only work their local area.

For as long as I can remember, being a salesman was the most unstable way for someone trying to make a living. It's said that every morning salespeople wake up, they are unemployed until they make a sale. They are hunters, not farmers. They have to hunt every day to survive. Otherwise, they will starve. The irony is that while the financial industry is a multi-trillion dollar industry, the big companies make the lion's share of the money, while the people working for them have to go to work every day to earn a living.

Time For A Change

We can build a predictable system in one of the largest industries in the world—the financial industry. In the past two decades, the System Builder, a new breed of entrepreneur, emerged who believes that it is possible to build a big organization using a duplicatable system.

Our ambition is to build a MD Factory, duplicating large numbers of Marketing Directors (MD). MDs are the System Builders of the financial distribution revolution. The System Flow is the system to turn our dream into a reality.

Our system helps entrepreneurs from all walks of life, with little or no experience, to build many MDs in different locations throughout the US, Canada, and eventually worldwide. If you have the dreams, we will provide you the vehicle.

"System Builder: The solution for building a big business!"

ENTERING THE SYSTEM

*"Find something you believe in and
put your life to fight for it!*

Do you know what you're getting yourself into? Someone invited you to look into a great opportunity. They are excited. You feel good about it. You make a decision to join.

Starting a new business takes an incredible amount of effort and usually costs a fortune to start up. Typically, one must find a new location, lease space, hire and train employees, experience setbacks, learn tricks of the trade, maintain pay rolls, track inventory, and so much more. Despite all that, the entrepreneur who starts a new business knows what he or she is getting into and is prepared for the challenges.

However, in this business many of us start out with much curiosity but with little preparation. Many people join our business suddenly, and thus they are not well prepared for the challenges they will face, nor do they understand how our system works. The unfortunate part is that few of them are willing to get started to learn or stay long enough to understand.

You Must Give Yourself Enough Time

It takes months to receive basic training. It takes two to three years to build a good team. And it takes at least five years to have a business in multiple locations and to build a solid foundation for your future.

You Are In Business For Yourself But Not By Yourself

The foundation of all good systems is its supporting architecture. In fact, great systems come with good instruction, planning, guidance, and continuous support.

Luckily, there are field trainers, leadership mentorship, home office back up services, regular training from product providers, classroom training as well as big events. All of these supporting structures exist to assist you in your new business venture. Thus new trainees will be in a strong position to learn the system and start running the system the day they join.

> **A system is a set of instructions and guidelines for the builder to follow to be able to move toward their goal successfully.**

You Must Be Disciplined

The system is useless until you follow it. You must have strong discipline to be a system builder. Discipline means that you must do the things that make you successful even though you may not like to do it.

You must have physical discipline. Most people start the business on a part-time or second-career basis. After a full day's work, you now add on extra hours to learn the business. The flesh may be weak, but your spirit must be willing to overcome this challenge.

> **The first 90 days you must be out in the field and attend all meetings to get familiarized with the system.**

Add to that the emotional challenges. Even harder than overcoming exhaustion are the rejection, the doubt, the criticism, and the negativity you will face from the people you come into contact with about the business. Many of these people are your friends, relatives, and people you care about. You must develop strong emotional discipline to maintain a positive attitude and move on with your business.

The Spirit Of The System

BELIEVE: Some people have to see to believe. Some believe before they see. The journey of a thousand miles begins with a single step. Belief is the first step. You must believe in your future. You must know deep in your heart that you will be successful, that you're destined to be great.

> *"To be a champ, you have to believe in yourself when no one else will."*
> –SUGAR RAY ROBINSON

TRUST: In a system built on people, trust is the number one ingredient you need to build a team. Living in a world of bad news, con men and scams, we learn to be hesitant and skeptical. Imagine how hard it would be to do anything if everyone in our team acted the same way. You won't be successful unless you learn to open up and trust the people you work with.

> *A fool is someone who trusts everyone. A fool is also someone who trusts no one. In your life, you must trust someone, sometime.*

The integrity of our system is the mutual investment of time. You invest your time to learn the business, and the trainer invests their time to teach you the business. They will become successful only if you become successful.

Have A Goal Of Greatness

*"Obstacles are those things you see
when you take your eyes off the goal."*
—HANNAH MORE

If you work the system, the system will work for you. But what is your expectation? What is your goal? Without a clear goal, most people will not be successful. The system is the vehicle, but you must provide the destination. You must fix in your mind your purpose for doing this business.

Many people want to be financially independent. However, few can say exactly the amount of assets needed to be considered wealthy and the target date to achieve it.

When you put your goals down on paper, you have a concrete plan. Take time to think about what you want in life. Then the system will be at your service.

"It's your life. Be specific!"

THE IMPORTANCE OF THE SYSTEM

*"If you want to be big,
you need to have a system."*

You Only Need A System If You Want To Be Big

If you want to do it small, you don't need a system. If you want to sell all by yourself, who cares about a system? But if you want something to duplicate and multiply—if you want something somebody can follow, not just you—then you need to have a system.

Unfortunately, a large number of people don't see themselves being big. Hence, they hardly pay any attention to a system.

Builders Love The System

It's clear that great builders of any kind—great coaches, great entrepreneurs, great engineers, great schools, great companies, great governments—all rely heavily on a workable, predictable system.

> *If you open one restaurant, you don't need a system.*
>
> *But if you want to open 10 restaurants, then you got to have a system.*
>
> *If you want to build thousands, you got to be a system builder.*

Great Achievement Should Be System-Driven Rather Than Personality-Driven

Small minds pay attention to personal skills and techniques. Big minds pay attention to the system. Thus, if you want to be big, you don't want talented people in your team. You want a system builder.

*"Would you rather be a 5-star chef or
the owner of a chain of McDonald's?"*

Does it mean that a strong-willed person with an attractive character won't be needed or do well? In fact, many of them do quite well. But if they make it because of their skill, talent and charisma, they're not duplicatable. People would say, "Look at the special strengths he possesses. Only he can do it." In such case, he appears to be above the system. Eventually, their growth will be limited.

> *"Most personality-driven businesses tend to be temporary and small."*

However, if he uses his inner strength to run the system, to be more duplicatable, he can do it bigger and faster. He can be a great duplicator.

The System Builder – The Ultimate Entrepreneur

Your main purpose is to build a large team and a big business, and you must build it through the system.

It's Tough To Build The System

Like a railroad track, it's a pain to build the track. But when it's done, it's easy to run on. Likewise, it's hard to set up a system in your hierarchy, but when it's set, the team can grow bigger, faster. Building a team that follows the system takes tremendous discipline and sacrifice.

Follow The System

You must master the system and follow the system religiously. If you want your team to copy you, you can't follow it once in a while. You must do it all the time.

> *"You must create a culture of discipline to follow the system."*

A System Creates Duplication And Multiplication

If your first generation duplicates you, your second generation will duplicate your first, and your third will duplicate your second, and on and on. That is duplication and multiplication.

"Systematize to multiply!"

Your Highway To Success

Building your business without a system is like driving a car without a map or directions. Hence, the system shows you step by step exactly what you need to do to arrive at your destination.

Without The System

- ▶ Confusion
- ▶ Frustration
- ▶ Chaos
- ▶ Internal Conflict
- ▶ Uncoachability
- ▶ Unteachability
- ▶ Discouragement
- ▶ Quitting

Submission To The System

The system is the product of thousands of people's efforts, many years of accumulated experience, and a few million mistakes. It has consistently been proven to be effective and has produced great success for many builders. Of course, no system is perfect—especially a system that intends to build people.

Don't try to change the system until you've understood and mastered it. That's like buying a McDonald's and tailoring it to your own tastes and style. Everything we do, the way we build—there is a reason behind it. Be a student of the business.

"You run the system. The system runs your business."

THE SYSTEM FLOW

"A simple solution for building a big business."

▶ A Powerful Growth Machine

▶ A Clear Focus System

▶ A Plan to Simplify and Multiply

▶ A Vast New Prospect Market

▶ An Explosion of Presentations and Production

▶ Predictable and Duplicatable

▶ Lowers Barriers for All Builders

▶ Easy to Monitor

▶ Goal Driven/Clear Aim for Next Step

▶ Wide - Deep - Exponential Growth

▶ A Fast, Efficient Way to Build a Big Base

▶ Train More Trainers

▶ Creates Urgency and Momentum

▶ Mobilizes Old and New Builders

▶ Fosters Teamwork

▶ Increases Taprooting

▶ Liberates Builders for Expansion

▶ And More…

"The more you do, the more you understand, the more you love it."

MD: THE PRODUCT OF OUR SYSTEM

"You must try to qualify for MD in 90 days."

All good things come with being a Marketing Director.

MD: The Ultimate Position

▶ You achieve the highest level in the system.
You also have the most accountability and responsibility,
like every leader and builder in the system.

▶ You start to run your own baseshop, your own business.
However, MD is a beginning, not the end. This is the
moment that you have to increase more personal activity,
field training, and leading by example.

▶ Your potential income is huge. Build a big base.

▶ The more MDs you build, the more secure your future
income will be. You must become a MD first
and duplicate the process to build a MD Factory.

*"MD is the final product of our system.
Thus either you're a MD or you're a MD-to-be."*

FOCUS ON MD

MD is your business. MD is your outlet. Your total focus is to identify, build, and lead a large team of MDs. Your daily activities should comprise of anything that helps you build new MDs. There will be big and small MDs, but those who have more MDs will be more successful.

Everyone must know the MD Guidelines. Everyone must follow the MD Checklist and know where they stand.

Keep it simple. Anyone who is serious about the business must get their license, qualify for MD Club, then qualify for MD as soon as possible.

THREE SIMPLE STEPS TO MD:

1. Submit License
2. MD Club
3. MD

If you have a chance to build outlets like McDonald's, the question is, "How many can you build, how fast can you build them, and how many cities should you build in?"

"Those who control distribution control the market. Builders who control large networks of MDs control the future."

7 STEP DUPLICATION

"7 & 7: Complete the 7 Steps in 7 Days."

1. Submit License

2. Meet the Spouse

3. Prospect List

4. Field Presentation BMP

5. Personal Financial Strategy

6. MD Club: 3-3-30

7. Duplication

"The perfect copy machine."

THE
PROSPECT LIST

*Your Fortune
List*

THE MD TRAINEE

"The raw material of the system"

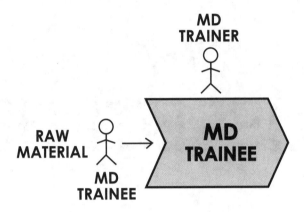

The Wrong Material

If you run a factory, it's critical to make sure the raw materials you bring to the factory are the right ones. For example, if you run a cake factory, you must have the correct ingredients. And not only must the ingredients be right, they must also be in the proper amount. Otherwise, the outcome will be a bad cake or no cake at all.

The same principles apply to our business. For example, how many times have you brought people into the business, and it turns out they do nothing or they hardly even start? Once? Twice? Ten times? A hundred times?

Why do some do, while most don't? Why do some cooperate and follow the system, yet others fail to submit to the system and complete simple tasks?

Who's At Fault?

When things go wrong, are the raw materials to blame or the factory manager who failed to bring in the right materials?

When people come in with the wrong attitude, is that because of them or because of the attitude of the person bringing them in? To a large extent we're the ones to blame.

Who Wants It?

Does the new person want this business more, or do you want him to be in the business more? Does the student want to learn more, or does the teacher want to teach more?

If the new person doesn't want it more than you, he won't do it based on his own will. He won't be proactive. He will be reactive. He will need to be motivated constantly.

Who's In Control?

When the trainer seems to have all the time in the world for the trainee, yet the trainee doesn't have time or doesn't make time, what kind of training can you provide?

Who Follows Whom?

Should the teacher follow the student, the coach follow the player, the trainer follow the trainee? Or should it be the other way around?

Look For The Right Material

1. LICENSE IS SUBMITTED RIGHT AWAY

No license, no business. What's the point of training a person when they don't even submit the paperwork to get licensed?

2. GET THE SPOUSE / FAMILY ON BOARD

If their partner or family is not supportive or even against the business, how much of a chance is there for them to survive long term?

3. SHARE A STRONG VISION, DEVELOP A GREAT PROSPECT LIST

Unless the couple sees the business, commits to develop a great prospect list and continues the commitment to build more names to dominate the market, it's likely they won't be successful in this business.

4. BOTH CAN GO OUT IN THE FIELD

Not only the trainee. If the spouse supports them in the business, they can both go out in the field as well as invite people for home business presentation meetings. This shows commitment and belief in the business. It's also critical that they learn and duplicate the business.

5. THEY BUY INTO THE MISSION

It's so important that they understand the financial concepts, the Personal Financial Strategy (PFS), and that they see how we help people. They must sell out to what we do.

"Something to believe in. Do they believe? Do you believe?"

> *Recruit the person who wants to join.*
>
> *Sell to the person who wants to buy.*
>
> *Build with the person who wants to build.*

THE PROSPECT LIST (PPL)

"The prospect list is where it all begins."

What's A PPL?

A PPL is a list of people who may or may not join you. It's also a list of people who may or may not buy from you.

Someone you think may join you may not, and someone you think may not join you may.

Set No Limits For Your PPL

▶ Shoot for at least 100 names. Everybody knows at least 200 to 300 people. Many people have more than that in their cell phone.

▶ Remind them this is just the beginning.

▶ Doing PPL is part of the job, a daily business routine.

▶ Highlight the top 25 prospects.

▶ Identify the first 5 people you will contact.

EVERYBODY IS A PROSPECT

▶ Every person you know is a prospect.

▶ Every person a prospect knows is a prospect.

▶ Every person you have ever met and will ever meet is a prospect.

▶ Every person who walks, talks, and breathes within 10 feet of you is a prospect.

PROSPECT LIST MENTALITY

*"You are one prospect list away
from an explosion."*

Most great builders are great recruiters, and, of course, great recruiters are great prospectors.

Create a habit of prospecting. You can never do the prospect list one time and be done with your business. You must eat, sleep, and breathe PPL until you become financially independent. By focusing on your PPL every day, your mind will work in miraculous ways to seek names for you.

> **REMEMBER:**
>
> *There will be times when you try to remember somebody and you can't think of their name right away.*
>
> *Yet a few days later, this name will pop up.*

It's so critical that you have a PPL mentality, that you duplicate it consistently to your teammates, and that they duplicate it to their teammates. Otherwise, your team won't survive.

*"You can never build a big team
unless every one of your team members
has a prospect list mentality."*

THE PROSPECT LIST IS YOUR INVENTORY

Have you ever gone to a restaurant with little food in the kitchen or to a grocery store with empty shelves? How about a repair shop with no parts?

If you own a restaurant or a grocery store, your inventory is food. If you run a repair shop, your inventory are parts.

We Are In The People Business

Our inventory is the prospect list, our lists of names. No new lists, no new names, no new inventory, and you're out of business.

▶ A typical person should always have a minimum of 50 names on a list at any given time to maintain activities.

▶ A typical baseshop should have 500+ names at any given time to have daily activities.

"The last time most people did the prospect list was a long, long time ago."

You cannot expect to go into this business and do PPL one time only. You cannot expect to be successful by just listing a handful of your friends and relatives. You must work relentlessly to come up with more names.

> **If your team is struggling, the first thing you need to do is check their prospect lists and then their agendas for appointments.**
>
> **You will find the answer to the problems very quickly.**

Prospecting Everyday

The key element of prospecting is regular contact with your prospects.

- Contact your prospects everyday.
- Follow up on your prospects everyday.
- Update your list everyday.

"You never know which name on that list will become your next superstar."

Have A Prospect List With You At All Times

"Don't go prospect. Prospect as you go."

- A name and a phone number should be written down ASAP. Your memory doesn't always give you a second chance.
- Great prospectors are always ready to write down names. They carry a small notepad, a prospect list, or a prospect book at all times.
- A notepad or a piece of paper will do the job, but the prospect book will keep and organize these names for the long term. It's your greatest asset. Keep it. Update it. Follow up.

"Maintaining a prospect list is like a businessperson looking into their balance sheet everyday."

You Get Paid To Prospect

Think about it this way. If you are licensed and you prospect 10 people and get 1 recruit, and assuming 1 recruit will generate 1 sale that is hypothetically worth $1000, then each prospect is worth $100, whether they join or not.

Thus, when you contact 1 person, if they say No, don't think as if you failed. Instead, think as if you gained $100. When you contact the 2nd person, think as if you gained $200. And when you contact the 10th person, think as if you will get 1 recruit and 1 sale. Mentally, this concept can help you prospect and contact people.

"Salespeople look for a sale to get paid.
Builders look for prospects to recruit.
When recruits come, the sales will follow."

Your Prospects Are Your Natural Market

In this industry, there are a lot of sales organizations buying leads or lists of names. They have to pay a good amount of money for these cold lists in hopes of making a sale.

On the other hand, most names on our prospect list are from our warm market, our natural circle of friends, relatives, and acquaintances.

Everyday in America and the world over, there are thousands of people contacting and calling people.

They don't worry about the Nos.

They just pay attention to the Yeses.

That is how they get paid.

The good thing about the warm market is the established relationships and trust. You can approach them easier and faster.

THE WARMEST LIST:

Sometimes called "the flat tire list". These are your closest people. You can call for help at any time, any place. They will be there for you, and you will be there for them. These are the people that you can drop by, stop by any time.

THE WARM LIST:
The people you know well. The people who would show up at family weddings and important events.

THE LUKEWARM LIST:
The larger circle of people you know—acquaintances, people you do business with and work with, people at church, parties, anybody whom you know their names and faces.

Can You Handle The "No"?

If you put one crab in the basket, it will climb out easily. But if you put a bunch of crabs in, none can escape because any crab attempting to climb out will be pulled back by many other crabs!

Welcome to the real world. New recruits will find out that the people closest to them will say "No" to them. Not only that, many of them will express doubt, negativity, and criticism.

> **Most people don't want change. They even don't want others to change. That is why in the great land of opportunity, most people would rather struggle everyday to make a living than find a way to make a fortune.**

3 WAYS TO DO PPL WITH A NEW RECRUIT

1. Hand Out A Top 25 List

If you hand out a Top 25 list to your new recruit and ask him to bring it back, he may never return. This person will think of endless reasons why his uncle, his sister, his cousin, his best friend, and his coworker would not join.

If the person does come back, the list he hands you is little more than a bunch of odd names and cold numbers. You might as well open the phone book and start dialing.

2. PPL In The Office Without The Spouse

If you do the PPL in the office without the spouse, you will get a limited list. Do this only if you don't have any other option or if you need to go out in the field right away.

3. PPL In The Home With The Spouse

Doing the PPL in the home with the spouse is by far the best way to do the prospect list. When you do the prospect list in the person's home:

▶ **THEY OPEN THE DOOR FOR YOU TO DO BUSINESS WITH THEM**

A SIMPLE RULE:
If I can invite this person into my home and he can invite me into his home, we could be in business together.

The minute a team member lets you into his home, sits you down at the kitchen table, and offers you a beverage, you know you're in business.

"What's the point of recruiting a person who would not trust you?"

▶ **YOU GET A CHANCE TO BUILD A RELATIONSHIP WITH YOUR NEW BUSINESS PARTNERS**

Take the time to get to know your team. Take a slow approach and go faster rather than take a fast approach and go nowhere. I'd rather have time for 5 people than have no time for 100 people.

"How can you retain people if you don't know them?"

Take the time to quantify your team's PPL. With your help, you can get more names from them than if they did the PPL without you.

Take the time to qualify your team's PPL. Knowing everybody well on the list gives you a better idea whom you'll have a better chance to do business with. Know their age, their job, their

"Why spend days to make a sale and not even spend one hour to get a prospect list? Why recruit a person and forget the PPL that can bring in 10 more?"

situation, etc. The more you know, the deeper connection you can make.

"Increase effectiveness, minimize failures."

▶ **YOU RECRUIT THE SPOUSE**

One of the biggest problems we have in this business is
the spouse who doesn't know what their partner is doing
all night. Defuse a bomb before it explodes.
Get to know the spouse. Show them what we do.
Sell them the dream. This builds great confidence
for the family. You never know. The spouse may be
more excited about the business than your team member.

▶ **YOU DOUBLE YOUR MARKET**

When you do the prospect list with both partners,
you enlarge your market twofold. You will get a
larger prospect list and a lot more referrals.

▶ **YOU CREATE A SHARED MARKET**

Their prospect list is also your prospect list.
Since they are on your team, it's your market too.
Even if they stop doing the business, those people
on the list may need your help. Thus, take time
to know the names on each list.

▶ **YOU FAST START THE COUPLE INTO THE BUSINESS**

As soon as you identify your top prospects,
have the couple call the ones who live nearby.
Take the couple out in the field immediately.
Once you've shown them how we do the BMP,
how we Bring the Meeting to the People, and
how we help families, you've just sold them the
dream all over again and locked them into
the business.

FIELD TRAIN PROSPECTING WITH YOUR TEAM

> ## WHICH IS MORE IMPORTANT:
> ▶ *Make 1 sale?*
> ▶ *Recruit 1 person?*
> ▶ *Get 100 names?*

Don't just go out with your people for field training sales and recruits only. Builders love to take their people out to prospect, contact, drop by, stop by, and especially to do the prospect list.

When doing the prospect list at a new recruit's home, take a team member with you. That way, you help both the new recruit and you also train your team member.

"You don't need to teach them how to recruit and build. Just do it. Your actions are worth a thousand words."

CREATE A FORTUNE LIST

Every time you add a name to your prospect list, you add to your fortune as well as to your prospects' fortunes. Who is so fortunate to be on your list?

"A prospect list can literally change your life."

DROP BY, STOP BY

"Contact many people many times."

One of the great secrets in our business is seeing people face to face. You can contact people through e-mail, phone call, or text message. But the most successful way to contact people is by meeting with them in person.

1. Drop By A New Prospect

Once you quantify and qualify the PPL, you can take the new recruit to drop by their top 5 prospects: their friends, relatives, and neighbors. Dropping by a prospect with the new recruit is the easiest way to share the opportunity.

▶ The "Flat Tire" List. I often ask new recruits what if they encounter an emergency situation, like getting a flat tire or catching the flu? Who are the top 5 people they would ask for immediate help? These people are very close to them and are also the easiest to drop by and share our story.

2. Doors Open

Contrary to what people fear, most prospects are very friendly and receptive. In the last 26 years of my career, I hardly

> *Normally, I do not call my friend to ask for "an appointment".*
>
> *I just ask, "Friend, are you home now? Great! I will just stop by for a short time. I have something great to show you!"*
>
> *Of course, if my friend is busy with something, he would tell me.*

experienced any bad situations. The worst thing that may happen is a prospect who says they're busy or it's not the right time. In most cases, though, we're invited in with open arms because the prospects are the friends, relatives, or neighbors of the new recruit.

3. Element Of Surprise

When I make phone contact, either I talk to the husband or the wife. Sometimes I talk to the wrong person. But when I drop by, quite often I am in for a surprise. When I think that the husband would be the one who is interested, I actually find out the wife is the one, or vice versa. Other times, neither the husband nor the wife are interested, but rather the brother-in-law, cousin, or aunt whom I meet at the house.

4. Keep It Short

▶ Don't stay too long. Let them know up front that you'll be there only briefly, for example, a half hour.

▶ Give a quick overview of our business. The key is to sell them the potential and invite them to our next business presentation meeting. If they're interested in our financial solutions, we'll schedule a Personal Financial Strategy appointment. We do not focus on recruiting or selling at the drop by.

▶ The odds for you to find a potential recruit are a lot higher. With a drop by, you can see 3 to 5 families a night.

5. Easier To Handle Objections

Seeing people face to face allows you to handle objections much easier than on the phone. They can see the conviction in your body language and the belief in your eyes. Also, they can't hang up on you.

Using the business review card is also helpful in these situations, and if there are any questions left, tell them our manager will be available to answer their questions.

6. Easier To Fast Start

A drop-by prospect, after joining, is much easier to upstart because we know them. We visited them at their home and became familiar with their family. We've developed a good relationship.

7. Duplication

Your new recruit will duplicate what you do. They'll love to drop by and bring their team out to do BMPs. They become "field friendly" from the outset. They love to be out in the field.

8. Drop By A Team Member's Home

Drop by to see not only new prospects but also existing team members as well.

▶ Visiting a current team member builds relationship. Know her family. Defuse some problems that may arise with the spouse. Impart a sense of urgency to the team. They will know that you are always out in the field and that you care for them.

▶ Drop by a former team member. Most people slow down or quit due to bad timing or temporary personal issues. Your visit can revive them. They can also give you referrals.

▶ Drop by a leader. You should always have time for your leader. Your leader should always have time for you. This is the person that will do or die with you in the long term. Drop by, appreciate her, and appreciate her family.

9. Drop By A Client

Most clients know you well. You have been to their home 2 or 3 times already. Just say you're in the neighborhood, that you wanted to drop by to say hello. Most of the time, they will be happy to see you and appreciate your visit.

Maintain a good relationship with your clients. They're one of your best sources of referrals for more prospects, more sales, and more recruits.

10. Drop By to Build, Rebuild Momentum

It only takes 30 relentless days of drop bys to build up speed. This is the most powerful way to build new legs, revive old legs, overlap leadership, and create a high level of personal activities, ultimately leading to an explosion.

"Drop by: A system whereby BMP never stops."

> *Personally, I love to do drop bys. I get to meet new people.*
>
> *I have a chance to meet both spouses. I get to see their home. I learn a lot about a couple by dropping by their home.*
>
> *I would never be able to do all this had I contacted the prospect on the phone.*

PROSPECTING AND CONTACTING WITH THE SURVEY CARD

In our business, we have several solutions to people's financial problems. But each person's situation is different. Some people are suffering badly and need help to solve the financial problem they are facing. Countless others are looking for an opportunity that will change their life. We are the ones who have the answer.

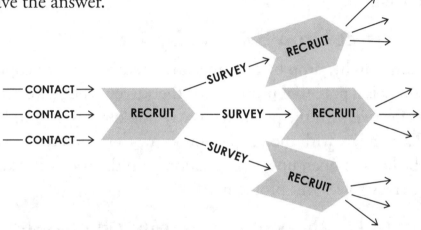

The financial survey card is the perfect vehicle to do the job. By conducting the survey, you can bring the message and the solution to the people directly. When people answer the questions, they give you feedback on what's important to them financially. You don't have to sell. You don't have to recruit. You simply offer vital information to those who need

ADVANTAGES OF THE SURVEY:

1. No pressure on the prospect to join or buy.
2. No pressure on the trainee/ trainer to recruit or sell.
3. Eliminates fear of recruiting/ selling or talking to people.
4. You see more people faster.

it without any pressure or demands. If they wish, they will let you know whether they want to learn more about the financial concept and products or if they're interested in the business opportunity.

Thus, prospecting and contacting become a lot easier, faster, and more duplicatable. You don't need to learn how to talk or what to say to people. The survey will do the job by itself. This can increase activities for both the new as well as the old team member.

The Perfect Drop By, Stop By Tool

You can stop by, drop by anytime, anywhere to survey people. Anybody is a potential prospect for the survey. The survey is very effective with the people you may not know well, and it works wonders with the people you know too. Sometimes, it can be hard to open up a conversation with the warm market. The survey solves this problem.

How To Do the Survey

Use the small flip chart with the survey.

If the prospect shows interest, make a return appointment or invite them to the BPM.

Ask the Trainer/MD to set the appointment, if appropriate.

MISSION POSSIBLE

- ▶ **3 surveys a day**
- ▶ **100 surveys a month**
- ▶ **10 personal recruits**
- ▶ **3 new MD Club**

"You can change your life and explode your business in 30 days."

*"Ask, and you will receive.
Survey, and you will get the answer.
Those who ask the most and survey the most
will recruit the most!"*

GETTING REFERRALS

Not all people will join or be interested in the business. But they can give referrals.

▶ **YOUR CLIENTS:** Your clients are a good source of referrals, but not the only one.

▶ **YOUR NATURAL MARKET:** A lot of your family, friends, relatives, and coworkers initially will not join or buy from you. But if you stay in the business, in time the referrals will come.

It's important that you always remain positive about your business and your products because they're watching you. No referrals will be given unless they see that you're happy with what you do.

In fact, some of your natural circle who did not support you when you started may change their minds and eventually want to help you.

▶ **YOUR ACQUAINTANCES:** You need to project an image of a successful businessperson, looking for more people to work with you and for you. A friend of your brother, the person who fixes your car, the cousin of your in-laws, a person you met at a wedding or a party—all these people may be interested or refer you to someone who might be.

How To Get Referrals?

Just ask for it.

I always ask my clients, my family members, and my

acquaintances to give names of people who would want to be in our business. I ask a lot of these "Who do you know...?" questions, and the results have been very rewarding.

> ## WHO DO YOU KNOW?
> ▶ *"Who do you know wants to make extra income?"*
> ▶ *"Who do you know wants to have a second career?*
> ▶ *"Who do you know is dissatisfied with their job?"*
> ▶ *"Who do you know is not happy with their business?"*

"Ask many people many times."

When To Follow Up On Referrals

As soon as possible.

A referred lead is red hot. If you don't follow up right away, you may put it off and forget about it. After you've followed up on a client's referrals, report back to your referrer. They really appreciate you for doing that, and if you were not successful, he or she may give you another lead that is better.

BMP + BPM

*Bring people
to the meeting,
and bring the meeting
to the people.*

BMP + BPM

"Bring people in. Send them out.
Keep them moving."

BPM: BRING PEOPLE TO THE MEETING

BMP: BRING THE MEETING TO THE PEOPLE

We bring the meeting to the people, then we bring people to the meeting, so that we can bring the meeting to more people, and on and on…

BPM is like an airline hub. BMP is like the flight. What's the hub without the flights? What are all the flights without the hub?

BPM + BMP must work together. We cannot run a system of BMP without BPM. And of course, BPM without BMP is very ineffective.

The more BPMs and BMPs you do, the more prospects, recruits, trainers, and builders you'll have. It's a system whereby prospecting and recruiting never stop.

When many operations started, they had lots of BMPs and home meetings. But when they got an office, they settled down and relied on BPMs only.

BMPs should generate guests for the BPM. And recruits from the BPMs will create activities for BMPs.

BPM Together With BMP

Ideally, you should BMP people first, and then bring them to the BPM. That way, they are informed and prepared before coming into the office. A person who sees the BMP and decides to go to the BPM will probably want to join.

On the other hand, many guests are often invited directly to the BPM. They tend to be reserved and conservative because they don't know what's going on.

That's why you need the second meeting, which is the business interview at the office. But if you cannot arrange that, then instead you could follow up the BPM with a BMP at their home. You can do the presentation, the business interview, and the sign up all at the same time.

THUS:

BMP ⇨ BPM

or

BPM ⇨ BMP

This approach is very effective, and you could meet the spouse, which can make the decision to join more solidified.

HOME BPM

There is more than one way to share the business opportunity. Besides doing the BPM at the office, doing a home BPM has many advantages and yields great results.

1. BRING IT CLOSE TO HOME: Sometimes, people live too far from the office. In such cases, it's much easier for guests to see the BPM at a location near their home.

2. TIME CONVENIENCE: The BPM at the office happens only on certain days and certain times. Home BPMs can be done any day and any time.

3. EASIER TO INVITE: The new recruit can invite friends, relatives, and neighbors to their home easier than to the office.

4. EASIER TO MEET THE HUSBAND AND THE WIFE: It's easier to get the couple together and show the presentation to them at home rather than at the office.

5. THE RECRUIT BECOMES MORE ACTIVE: The new recruit takes charge of the business because it is done in her home. She tends to be passive and less involved when she goes to the office.

6. EASIER TO TRAIN AND DUPLICATE MORE PEOPLE: When doing home BPMs, bring team members to help. They'll learn faster by observing and practicing.

7. BEST WAY TO EXPAND / BUILD LONG DISTANCE: Most long distance building starts with home BPMs.

"A team that has more home BPMs has more recruits, more duplication, and more leaders."

MORE AND MORE PEOPLE GO OUT IN THE FIELD, MORE AND MORE PEOPLE GO TO THE BIG EVENT

ATLANTA CONVENTION, 2002

Can you monitor these two numbers? How many team members go out in the field, and how many team members go to the big event?

A lot of people fill out the paperwork and think they're in the business. You're not in the business until you're out in the field every night.

For you to build the business, you have to ask, "Besides you, who else goes out in the field?"

When you call someone and their spouse says they're out in the field, that's when you got it made, when your downline goes out in the field without you having to remind them.

But going out in the field in the local area is just the first test of discipline of an entrepreneur. The real test is getting people to the big event because this is the test that most people fail. Most people want to make money, but they don't want to go to the meeting.

Many people can go to big events in the local area, but once you put it a little far away, then you find out the real truth. The problem is when you have the event close by, they show up late, and when they show up, they don't listen. But if you put the event far away, usually they show up early and they do study. It's funny. I don't know how to explain that, but that's the way it is.

You can only build people this way. You build people by having them go out in the field every night, and you build people by having them go to the big event, because through the big event they are built.

I don't want to build people. I don't want to train people. People, you cannot tell them to do anything. But at the big event, they listen, and they listen to somebody else.

All you have to do is find the right kind of people. But you can never find the right kind of people. You just got to find a lot of people and let them go out in the field and see if they go to the big event, and the system will help them or eliminate them.

THE SIMPLE PRESENTATION

"The Secret of the BMP"

The whole purpose of the BMP is to make it duplicatable. Your people must be able to copy you in a short period of time. They must say to themselves, "It's so simple, I can do it!"

1. Short

We don't want to be there all night. The presentation should be between 30 to 60 minutes. What good is it if you spend 3 hours to recruit a person only to have your trainee depressed by the difficulty of recruiting and the amount of information they need to learn to do the job?

2. Simple

We want the new person to be able to memorize the presentation and duplicate us fast. Most people should be able to repeat your presentation after the third viewing.

3. Don't Answer Questions

The purpose of the BMP is to share the good news about our financial concepts and our business opportunity. We don't plan to recruit or to make a sale. If they like the business, we invite them to our BPM. If they like the financial solutions, we schedule them to see one of our licensed experts to do the PFS.

If they have any further questions, we refer them to see our manager.

4. Speed

Since it's short and simple, we can see many people in one night.

5. Duplicatable

In 7 days, trainees should be able to do the presentation by themselves. Since it is short and simple and since they don't have to handle questions or objections, trainees should have no fear going out in the field on their own.

"After 7 days, are your people
ready to go out and do presentations,
or are they still calling you to
take them out?"

> ## A "SICKENINGLY SIMPLE" PRESENTATION
> *Personally after watching the simple presentation 3 or 4 times, I felt very itchy to present it myself. By the time I watched 8 of them, I was able to remember just about every line, every transition, every word. Listening to the simple presentation over and over made me sick. I almost couldn't stand it anymore and couldn't wait to go out and do it myself.*

SHARE YOUR STORY – SELL YOUR COMPANY'S STORY

"The best presentation is your story."

Imagine you just came back from a wonderful vacation in Europe and shared pictures of your trip to a group of friends. You show off slides of beautiful churches, castles, monuments and scenery, but you are not to be found in any of the photos.

What a loss. People can probably find the same pictures of these places in books or magazines. What your friends are most interested in is how you enjoyed the trip, your feelings about the journey, the food, the people you met, and the memorable moments you had. Pictures of you and the expression on your face are worth a thousand words.

"The low level law is to do the presentation. The high level law is to share the story."

Over the years, I found that sharing your story is the best presentation. When you show people our business, begin with your story on why you got involved and how you fell in love with the business. And before you end the presentation, make sure you share how this business impacts your life, how it makes a difference for your family as well as other families.

Every great company has a great story. Remember the story of Ray Kroc, the ice cream machine salesman, and how he discovered McDonald's? How about Starbuck's Howard Schultz, drawn into the Seattle coffee house by its aroma.

THE TRUE POINTS OF YOUR PRESENTATION ARE:
- ▶ Selling the belief in the Mission
- ▶ Selling the belief in the Vision
- ▶ Selling the belief in the System

It's your story and your company's story that attract and connect with people. Your story is unique, interesting, and sincere. When you tell your story, it makes you more comfortable, and it makes your guests more comfortable.

PSYCHOLOGY OF THE PRESENTATION

When it comes to the presentation, it's not about the details. It's the reason behind it.

When you do the presentation, you don't just sell the business, you sell your belief. When you go through concepts such as the X Curve, you are not only talking about financial solutions but really how they can make a positive difference for families, and especially your own family.

When you talk about a vision of a new industry, what you are literally doing is selling them your vision, your belief in how you see yourself and this company becoming very successful in the future.

MY FIRST 8 BMPS

I saw the opportunity in May 1985 at a Saturday morning BPM. I made an appointment for noon the next Monday. I was so excited I joined right away, bought the product Tuesday, and went out in the field that same night to do BMPs. I started right. I scheduled 3 appointments for the first night because the trainer insisted on a minimum of 3 appointments to go out with me.

The first appointment was at my brother-in-law's home. He is so close to me, so I knew he would do business with us. But to my surprise he did not. Then, I took my trainer to the home of my best friend, a sophisticated engineer. He did not show any reaction to the presentation. He was stone-faced the entire time and never even said a word, not even a No. At the third appointment, another friend showed some interest but wanted to think it over.

I was stunned. I thought all 3 of them would be very receptive, or at least 1 would, but not even 1 responded positively. I told my trainer that tomorrow will be better and kept apologizing for the first 3 failures.

The next day, I brought my trainer to 3 more places, and again, nobody showed any interest, just a few questions and remarks. I was so disappointed. We've been to 6 houses already.

I had to do something the 3rd night, but I couldn't get 3 appointments. I only had 2. I called my trainer and asked her to give me another chance and apologized because I could only find 2 appointments. Again, nothing came out of those 2 appointments.

My first 8 BMPs were all failures. I was so mad I almost wanted to quit. I did not understand why the closest people to me all said "No" or "I want to think about it".

But I couldn't quit. The thought of being a social worker for the rest of my life was even more painful. Also, I thought that we did good BMPs. In fact, we did everything right. After I thought about it, I realized there was no problem with our business or our presentation. It was their problem. I swallowed my pain and went on.

The first year in the business, I was bad, but I learned a lot. I learned that this business is not as easy as I thought. I learned that even brothers, best friends, and cousins will not do business with me. I learned to move on and to stay excited, even while being hurt. I learned that it was critical to go out as a team—me and the trainer—so we can motivate each other to keep going on. I did not take this business for granted, and I prepared myself for a long fight toward my independence.

> ## BUILDER'S NOTE:
> *Although all 8 BMPs were not successful, one very positive thing came out of it.*
> *I was duplicated! I saw 8 simple presentations over and over again. I memorized it by heart. I was able to do it myself. There was no real secret.*
> *Another interesting note: Most of these people eventually either joined or bought from me.*
> *Some did so a few months later on, while others took a year. The rest is history.*

WHAT IS "SELLING THE DREAM"?

THIS IS WHAT WE SELL:

- ▶ Be Somebody
- ▶ Be My Own Boss
- ▶ Own My Own Business
- ▶ Control My Destiny
- ▶ Great Income
- ▶ Financial Security
- ▶ Provide for My Family
- ▶ Do Great Things for People
- ▶ Travel Nationwide and Worldwide
- ▶ Build a Nationwide and Worldwide Business

"Don't sell them your dream. Sell them the dream that is most important to them."

YOU SHOULD HAVE BPMS REGULARLY

We need to do the BPM at least once every 3 to 4 days because:

- ▶ When people are prospecting, inviting, doing the BMP and recruiting, they need to bring these new guests or team members to the office as soon as possible.

- ▶ Just like a car, which needs to be refueled regularly, our teammates need to be recharged, energized, and motivated after being beat up in the field.

- ▶ Our trainers and trainees need to be recognized for their efforts and to share their success stories. They can also share their experiences of what it's like to be a crusader and how they make a difference for families.

- ▶ Regular BPMs are predictable and convenient for leaders, teammates, upline, and downline to meet with each other to train, plan, and share crucial information.

▶ If you do BPMs only once a week, the cycle of business slows down tremendously. It will be harder to find and build serious and committed people.

"What would you do if your car ran out of gas and you had to wait the whole week before you could get it refueled?"

BUILDER'S NOTE:

Don't ever miss a meeting.

Don't ever miss the BPM.

Don't ever show any sign of tiredness or lack of enthusiasm in the BPM.

Your team will recognize it and won't show up.

DAYTIME BPM

For so long we did meetings during the evenings and weekends, assuming that most people have to go to work. We forgot that there are a lot of people who would prefer to do our business on weekdays during regular working hours. So by doing the BPM in the day time, we attract a bigger, more diversified market.

> " The more BPMs, the more potential recruits, and thus the bigger the market you penetrate. "

Stay-At-Home Parents

Many stay-at-home parents have free time from morning until about 3pm, when their children come home from school. One of Japan's largest securities companies built the majority of their sales force with stay-at-home parents.

Day People

Many people feel more comfortable going to meetings and doing the business during the day rather than at night.

People Working At Different Shifts

Nurses, students, teachers, food service personnel, factory workers, and others may be busy working at night.

Professionals / Self Employed

CPAs, lawyers, doctors, real estate agents, and others have flexible schedules and may prefer daytime business meetings.

Unemployed / Between Jobs

These people are free during the day.

Regular Employed People

If it's important enough, people can ask for some time off from work to come see the business.

And More...

J.O.B. – THE JOURNEY OF THE BROKE

Most employees work only hard enough so that they won't be fired. And most employers will just pay them enough so that they won't quit.

MOZONE: THE ENVIRONMENT TO RECRUIT AND BUILD

"MoZone: The Momentum Zone.
It's an environment of energy, positivity,
excitement, and power!"

It's all about the atmosphere. In any entertainment center where there are crowds—a restaurant, a shopping mall, a show business—the environment is critical.

When people feel good, they do good. When people feel intimidated or re-served, they tend to close their minds.

> ❝ **BUILDER'S TRAP:**
>
> *A positive environment shouldn't be artificially "plastic fantastic".*
>
> *It must be natural and sincere. So don't overdo it.* ❞

Thus, always maintain a positive environment in the office, especially during the BPM. The BPM is show time for our business. It's our opening days. It's show off day for one of the best businesses and careers in the world!

"It pays to smile,
to be excited, and to be positive.
What a business!"

THE 10 COMMANDMENTS OF MOZONE

1. SIT IN FRONT

2. EYE CONTACT

3. WALK FASTER

4. TALK LOUDER

5. SMILE

6. DRESS SHARP

7. COME EARLY, STAY LATE

8. DECLARE YOUR INTENTIONS PUBLICLY

9. RAISE UP, STAND UP

10. STUMBLE FORWARD, STAY CONFUSED

"It's what's inside of you that counts."

10 WAYS TO
BUILD YOUR CONFIDENCE

1. Sit In Front

When I was a kid, I sat in the front row of the class. As I got to high school, I eventually moved to the middle. And by the time I went to college, I found myself somewhere in the back of the room.

Ever since, I always took a back seat in my life. I always sat in the back, hid behind someone else, lost myself in the crowd. In most situations, I was content and sometimes happy about it. Nobody bothered me. Nobody looked at me or said anything to me. But that came with a price. I realized that I was not winning.

> *"In a dogsled, if you're not the lead dog,*
> *the scenery doesn't change much."*

As a short guy sitting in the back, I gave up a lot. I didn't see most things ahead, except for other people's hair. I was passive, non-engaged, and frustrated. I was behind, and I found out most people were like me.

In our BPM, for instance, if we set 10 rows of chairs, most people will come in and start sitting down at the 10th row first. And if we set 3 rows, they will sit in the 3rd row. Very few people come in and sit in front. Even team members prefer to sit in the back.

One day, when reading *The Magic of Thinking Big* by Dr. David J. Schwartz, who suggested some simple techniques to build confidence, it hit me like a ton of bricks. I realized what went wrong! I made an effort to change. "I will sit in front from now on," I told myself. What a big change! It looked easy, but it's not that easy to do. Being a front-seater will change your life. You will be fully engaged. You will be a student of the business. You will be coachable.

When you sit in front, you take charge. You're at the front line. You listen more attentively. You have no distractions. You're totally focused. Your business mindset rises to a new level.

> *"Great leaders always sit in front, fight for the front, and are always ready."*

Sitting in front will lead your life down the winner's track. Not sitting in front could cost you and your team tons of money.

2. Eye Contact

I was a shy kid who was afraid to talk to people, let alone look into their eyes. People told me it's not polite to look into older people's eyes. The fear of people grew inside me. I could sit next to another person at a party for hours without saying a word, as if I was playing a silence endurance contest. Not surprisingly, I didn't feel too good about myself.

When I first started, this business was so uncomfortable for me. I had to contact people. I had to say something and look at people. But over the years, that was one of the best things that could have happened to me.

I learned to look straight in people's eyes. I could see through them. I could communicate with them. More often, eye contact speaks louder than words.

> *"Making eye contact establishes trust, confidence, and positivity with the person you communicate with."*

Now, I feel a lot more effective meeting people face to face rather than talking with them on the phone. I'm confident and more comfortable with people as a result.

3. Walk Faster

Your actions and your feelings go together. When you're sad, you walk slow. When you're happy, you walk faster. When you walk faster, you tend to be happier.

The environment you're in will also affect your actions and your feeling. When you listen to upbeat music, you are active and you move quicker. A sad song will slow you down. Even my car can recognize that. When I am sad, my car drives slow. But when I'm excited, my car gains speed.

Most of us wait until we feel good before we do something. Running a business based on our feelings is dangerous. The renown basketball star Jerry West said, "You can't get much done in life if you only work on the days when you feel good."

We can control our feeling. We can control our actions. We can control our life. Just walk faster. You'll find yourself a happier, more positive person.

> *"Hurry up! Get the job done.*
> *There are so many of things in life*
> *waiting for you to do, to see,*
> *and to enjoy."*

4. Talk Louder

When you're sad or tired, you talk in a low voice. When you are energetic and happy, you speak louder.

In fact, when you communicate, it doesn't matter much what you say. What matters most are the tone of your voice, the expression on your face, and the posture of your body.

> **It's said that the impact of communication comes:**
>
> *55% from body language*
> *38% from the tone of your voice*
> *7% from verbal content*

Just raise your voice one notch, you will feel stronger.

"Every time I call home,
my wife can tell right away if I had a
good day or a bad one."

5. Smile

"The world's best way to communicate."

A smile affects people more than anything else. A smile builds quick confidence and changes the environment around you.

One day at the doctor's office, most people seemed to be quiet, sad, or worried—until a lady came in with her child. The minute the kid smiled, the atmosphere in the waiting room lit up. Everyone smiled, became happy, and began to talk to each other. Amazing what a smile can do.

"When you smile, you change your attitude,
and you change the attitude of the people around you."

6. Dress Sharp

I used to dress down very casual and was proud of it. It seemed as if I wanted the whole world to know that I'm a social worker, I'm poor, I'm carefree, I'm taking it easy.

I got what I wanted. Nobody paid attention to me. Nobody took me seriously. Nobody talked any business with me. One of my cousins joined the business for months and never bothered to recruit me. One day, after I joined another person, I met him at a meeting. His first words were: "I never thought that you would want to be in business?!"

Having a habit of dressing up and looking sharp changed my outlook on life.

> *"If you dress up, you move up.*
> *If you dress down, you move down."*

When you dress sharp, you feel better and look more professional. People don't want to follow a sloppy-looking leader. Your appearance is very important. But don't be too formal or flashy. It may intimidate our guest, our client, or our potential business partner. You should also ask your guest to dress properly. The BPM is a business meeting. But don't be too strict, especially with a first-time guest.

7. Come Early - Stay Late

Most people come to the office on time or a little late, as if they go to work. On a BPM night, they come in, unprepared, lost in the crowd, hoping that their guest is somewhere in the MoZone area, hoping that their trainer won't be disappointed, hoping that their teammates won't get mad at them. I know. I was one of them.

The day I happened to come to the meeting an hour early, I saw a totally different scene. I saw a lot of work to prepare for. The chairs, the microphone, parking, the sound system, training schedules, name tags, sign-in sheets, upstart kits. I saw a business at work!

The minute the BPM ends, most people head to the parking lot and go home. I was one of them. Just like in any job, can't wait to get out. Just like in any classroom, can't wait for the bell to ring.

"I'm tired, I'm hungry, and I want to go home."

However, when I got home, most of the time I did nothing special like watching TV or reading magazines for hours.

Then, one day, I decided to stay late. I saw a totally different picture. The meeting after the meeting, setting goals, getting commitments, leaders staying after the meeting to help serious people create a business plan, monitor activities, and do paperwork.

After the meeting, people open up, the serious builders stay late, and the team goes out for a snack. It's their time to build relationships. They talk about the business in an informal way. They share a lot of insight and observation on how to improve each other's business.

"When you come early and stay late, you're in control. You're in the business."

Successful businesspeople show up to work early. Successful system builders master this challenge. Since you go the meeting anyway, why don't you come early, stay late, and spend an extra hour at the office? This extra hour gives you an entrepreneurial mentality that most employees hardly ever get to know!

8. Declare Your Intentions Publicly

You can't change or hit your goal unless you declare it and let many people know. For example, it's easier to quit smoking if you let everyone around you know your intention. If you have a goal, declare it. The goal is half done.

9. Raise Up, Stand Up

When it comes to some challenge or task, many people can hardly stand up or raise up. For many of us, the last time we raised our hand or stood up was in high school. Even if people raise up, they can hardly raise their hand high, pass their head. And even if they stand up, they can hardly stand up long enough.

It seems like people go through life carrying too much baggage. They were put down too many times. They got shafted by their boss, pulled down by their coworker, or criticized by their family. Their shoulders get heavy, their body worn out. Raising up is hard to do.

> *"Stand up for something you believe in.*
> *Raise up to your dream."*

10. Stumble Forward, Stay Confused

Many employees stumble forward easily when their boss gives them orders. They proclaim, "I can do it! I'll find the solution!" But when they have to work for themselves, they become shaky and hesitant.

Moving forward may seem risky, but doing nothing is even riskier. You can't wait until you know everything before you do something. You can't wait until all conditions are right before you start something.

"Success is never convenient."

Before success, you must fail. Those who never try never learn. Your activities create knowledge, but your knowledge won't create activities.

I often hear: "Show me everything. When I get all my licenses, I'll do it, big!" Unfortunately, that rarely happens! Usually these people don't even last long enough to get licensed.

"Action fights fear. Inaction creates more fear.
Walk right through your fear,
and the death of fear is certain."

MISTAKES TO AVOID AT THE BPM

Showing Up On Time

"If you show up on time,
you're too late."

If you show up on time, you're too late. You and your guest will have missed the whole point of the BPM: the Magic of MoZone. As a rule of thumb, teammates should be at the office at least a half hour before the meeting, and leaders should be at the office at least an hour before the meeting.

Bringing A Bad Day To The BPM

When you walk into the office, please leave your troubles behind. I know that life is tough out there, but we are in the people business. People at the office don't need to know about personal problems, traffic jams, or bad weather.

Our business is selling happiness, a "can do" spirit, a chance to make dreams come true. So when you enter the office, show that you're happy about what you do. Show that you're determined to be successful.

Waiting For Guests In The Parking Lot

Do not show that you are so desperate. If guests can find the parking lot, they can find their way into the office.

Either You're In Or You're Out, But Don't Hang Around

When you're at a meeting, stay in the meeting.

The BPM hours are your working hours. It's your job to learn from other trainers, to work the system, and to build your business. It is not a time to hide in the office and use the computer or go outside and talk on the phone. Your team may duplicate that. Other teams may duplicate it. You not only hurt your business; you end up hurting other people's business as well.

> ## MONKEY BUSINESS
>
> *"Monkey see, monkey do."*
>
> *In the duplication business, your people duplicate what you do, good or bad. And your people always do more than you.*
>
> *When you come 5 minutes late, your people come 10 minutes late.*
>
> *When you don't show up for 1 meeting, your people don't show up for 3 meetings.*
>
> *If you don't show up for one month, your people don't show up forever.*

Acting Casual To A First-Time Guest

Every time one of your guests walks out of the BPM room, you have to be excited, even if you've listened to the BPM thousands of times already. You cannot act casual. You have to treat every guest like your first. Don't ever forget where you come from. Do you remember the first time you saw the presentation? Wasn't that powerful?

Asking What They Think

When the BPM is over and you meet with your guests, what you say to them is so crucial. Instead of asking them what they think, can you say something positive and affirmative? Can you say, "Is that powerful? Was that a great presentation? This is an incredible opportunity, right? The presenter is very good, right?" This is why you recommended them to see it in the first place.

Doing The Business Interview Before The Business Interview

Sometimes your guest is excited and curious to know more about the business and begins to ask questions. And you, also excited, begin to answer their questions. You do your upline's job too early. You do the business interview before the business interview.

Instead of answering their questions, can you say, "Wonderful. Those are great questions. I'm glad you're interested. Write them down. I'm sure when you come back tomorrow to see my Marketing Director, she will answer all your questions."?

> **REMEMBER:**
>
> *Don't talk too much.*
>
> *Especially when you're not ready, when you don't know how to answer, or when you're not in control of the situation.*

*"The presentation in the BPM is to recruit.
The presentation in the parking lot is to destroy."*

Not Using The Business Review Card

The business review card is simple, clear, and convenient. We show the presentation, share the information, and they make the decision.

It's also very duplicatable. Everyone can do it. Just give them the card. Either they want to take a look at the business, or they want to understand more about our financial concepts and solutions. They tell us what they want.

MAKING APPOINTMENTS FOR THE BUSINESS INTERVIEW

Work With Your MD/Trainer To Set Up An Appointment

Understand that your MD/Trainer is not making an appointment for herself but rather for you. Do yourself a favor. Don't side with your guest and say he's too busy to make an appointment. Your MD understands that your guest has a job and a family. But you need to encourage him to meet with your trainer within 24 to 48 hours during the daytime. We need to talk to the guest while they're still excited.

Hold The Business Interview Within 24 To 48 Hours

If you don't set up an appointment within 24 to 48 hours of the BMP/BPM, the odds for the prospect to come back for the business interview are low. When a typical guest goes home, he will talk to his spouse, his cousin, and his friends. These people are going to rain on his parade with all sorts of negative comments: "You can't sell… There's no way you can do this…" etc. That's why the sooner we see them, the better chance we have of answering their questions and eliminating their doubts.

Do The Business Interview At The Office

Normally, when you do the business interview in the office, you have more control. But if you have guests at the BPM who don't show up for the business interview, they probably got shot down by the doom-and-gloom crowd. In that case, you can follow up the BPM with a BMP and recruit them at their house.

Follow Up

Follow up for good measure. Call him up to remind him about the appointment. If you sense he has been negatively affected by his friends or family, offer to give him a ride to the appointment and reassure him that this is a legitimate and worthwhile business opportunity.

THE BUSINESS INTERVIEW

"The proper interview."

The main purpose of the second interview is to recruit new team members, offer them an opportunity to start a new business, and be part of a successful system. They must know that they are joining a strong leader and a winning team. As always, keep it simple.

Things You Need To Remember For The 2nd Interview:

▶ At the interview, require the team member to be present with the return guest. He must learn to duplicate you.

▶ Inquire about their background.

▶ Review the flipchart again (5 min).

▶ Ask them:

"Have you ever been in a leadership role or business owner role before? Do you plan to develop one?"

"What is it about our message and our business that intrigues you?"

"Do you plan to do something big or special with your life?"

"Do you have any immediate needs to fulfill or urgent desires to achieve at this moment? For example, pay off debt, have your spouse stay at home?"

"Do you plan to be a part of a demanding, strong organization to build a business?"

▶ Answer basic questions.

▶ Tell them that most questions will be answered through field training and by our office training program.

▶ Take charge of your training program.
Tell them: "I'll see you tonight at 7pm at your home to get started. By the way, it will be an honor to meet your spouse. Can you have dinner early before I arrive?"

"The second interview is not just to sign them up. It's to fast start them.

> *Remember, this is not a lengthy classroom training.*
>
> *It's a step to move them toward a fast start.*

PERSONAL FINANCIAL STRATEGY

First, you must understand,

then you have a plan,

and you work your plan.

PERSONAL FINANCIAL STRATEGY (PFS)

After a person joins, we need to sit down with that person and their spouse to take care of their family with a personal financial strategy.

1. They Need To Understand Our Concepts and Products

The reason we grow is because we provide such badly needed information and services to Middle America. From proper needs for protection to long term investments, from managing debt to increasing cash flow, from creating an emergency fund to preserving their estate, every one of these concepts can change lives and their family's lives for generations to come. I remember when I first saw the X-Curve and the Rule of 72, I thought it was the eighth wonder of the world.

2. They Need To Be Helped

People don't need to buy our products to work for our company. But it's critical that they know information about and solutions to their personal finances. They need to know their current situation and what they should do to take care of their family's financial security. And if they have the need and are suitable, they should own the appropriate products as soon as they can.

3. They Need To Believe In Our Mission

The best way to help new recruits understand what we do for the consumer out there is to see how it helps them first. Practice what you preach. Help people understand and believe in building a strong financial foundation. It's easier for them to be successful in a business that they believe in and that does good things for people.

4. Share, Don't Sell

A normal salesperson would sell anything the consumer wants to buy, even if that salesperson doesn't own the product. Crusaders share what they believe in and recommend to others what they would do for themselves. You don't really need to sell. That's why we join, we own, and we share.

WHAT'S A CRUSADER? WHAT'S OUR MISSION?

"Do it right. Do it with pride."

We use the words crusade and mission often. What do they mean in our business?

Our mission is to make a difference for families by helping them build wealth for themselves and for other families. Our crusade is to share with people our financial concepts, so they can increase their cash flow, manage their debt, create an emergency fund, provide proper protection for the family, build long-term assets, and preserve their estate. Now more than ever, people need to understand how money works, have a financial goal, and begin to build a financial foundation for their future.

> *Our mission is to make a difference for families, to help build wealth for families.*

A crusader is someone who believes in what he or she is doing. They do the right thing. It also means that when they sell a product, they make sure that their clients understand all the advantages as well as the disadvantages of the product. The clients will only buy if it is good and suitable for them and their family. Likewise, when we recruit new members, we must tell them the advantages as well as the challenges of the business.

Crusaders die hard. When you have a good cause and a strong belief, you do it until you fulfill your mission. It is so good to be in a business where you can make a significant difference for families. With the stroke of your pen, you can protect the family, help their children save for college, and deliver retirement benefits, long term care, and peace of mind when tough times come.

THE 4 DIMENSION FLOW

1st Dimension	MD TRAINEE	MD CLUB	MD	MD FACTORY
2nd Dimension	PEOPLE GATHERING	THE BIG PUSH	THE BASE SHOP BUILDING MACHINE	THE HIERARCHY BUILDING MACHINE
3rd Dimension	CRUSADE	DREAM	TEAM BUILDING	WINNING
4th Dimension	TRUST	BELIEVE	COMMIT	FOLLOW

UNDERSTAND THE FIRST BLOCK OF THE MD FACTORY

I. The First Dimension

"DO IT RIGHT"

MD TRAINEE

"DO IT WITH PRIDE"

"People Gathering"

FAST START
JOIN - OWN - SHARE

- Start Licensing
- Develop a Prospect List
- Match-Up for Field Recruiting (BMP+BPM)
- Finalize your Personal Financial Strategy

7 STEP DUPLICATION

"7 & 7: Complete the 7 Steps in 7 Days."

1. Submit License
2. Meet the Spouse
3. Prospect List
4. Field Presentation BMP
5. Personal Financial Strategy
6. MD Club: 3-3-30
7. Duplication

"The perfect copy machine."

II. The 2nd Dimension: People Gathering

Why do you have to do prospect list, go out in the field to do BMP or invite people to the BPM, and do the PFS?

The purpose is to gather as many people as possible to join our business, and, of course, to bring in as many potential MD trainees.

When you join, you should gather at least 3 people to qualify for MD Club.

III. The 3rd Dimension: The Crusade

In the first block of the system, during the early stages of the business, the new MD trainee must see the goodness of the business, what we do to help people. It should be the mission, not the commission or the money, that impresses them.

IV. The 4th Dimension: Trust

We have to establish a relationship and develop the trust factor. That's the reason why we come to the MD trainee's home to talk to the spouse. If the couple doesn't trust us, it will be difficult to get them started.

V. The 5th Dimension: Duplication

Everything we do in the first block will be duplicated. Either we duplicate good or we duplicate bad. Either we do it right or we do it wrong. Whether we make it complicated or we keep it simple, the trainee will copy us. Like most things in life, the first step is so crucial. We may not have a second chance.

By the end of the 1st block, usually after the first 7 days, the new MD trainee will draw one of two conclusions:

1. "Wow, it looks good. It looks simple. It seems doable. I can do this!" With this mindset, things will start out great.

2. "Gee! It's all quite confusing. I need to learn more. I'm not sure if I can do it..."

If he has the latter thoughts, there will be a long, hard road ahead, and he may not make it at all.

THE 4TH DIMENSION

"Without trust from the family,
you cannot get a person to move."

The Trust Factor

It's a pain to work with somebody who doesn't trust you. How in the world does somebody join you one day and 3 days later on disappear? How does somebody listen to you one day and the next day doesn't believe a word you say? Something happened in between.

The Hidden Reason

In many cases people quit not because of the product or market conditions, but because of their spouse. Without support from the spouse, succeeding in this business is a losing battle.

Solve This Problem Early On

The minute a new person joins, tell them, "I need to see you and your spouse tonight at your home. Can you please finish dinner early, so we're ready to talk about business?"

If she asks, "What for?" You answer, "To get you started." The minute she says yes, she trusts you enough to let you in her home.

Gain Trust, Present The Business

The reason you need to go to her home is to gain trust and show the business to the spouse. If the spouse is busy, you should wait until they're available. Or if he can't see you, you should reschedule. You want them to know you're serious about this business.

> *Have you ever known a woman who lets her husband go out every night and she doesn't know what he's doing? It happened to me.*
>
> *The first few weeks I went out in the field, my wife received a call from a cousin telling her she saw me driving around with another woman.*

When both husband and wife agree to sit down with you, that's when you talk to them, because you need to explain the business to both of them. You should not explain only to one of them and let the one explain to the other. Both don't have to do the business, but both need to believe in what we do.

The Only Way To Build Is With A Couple

The short time you spend with the couple is the best investment you'll ever make with them. You'll find out right away if this is the family you're going to work with, or if there's no hope.

No Trust, No Work

The minute they trust you, they give you a good prospect list. And when they trust you, they don't mind taking you to see those people.

But if they don't trust you, they're not going to give you a real prospect list. Instead they hand you a list of people who—whether they join or not—don't affect them.

Get To Know The Real Family

At the home you meet the real family. At the office they are different people. But at the home they're real people, comfortable at their own place.

Make A Good First Impression

You come to their home, and the first impression is a good one. You show them a real business. You're committed. You care. You're serious. You're a person with a mission and a dream. You believe in what you do. You're absolutely positive. Your new recruit and her husband are fired up. The first appointment at her home determines the rest of her career, because at the first appointment she feels like rainbows.

Build It Right From Day One

The new recruit joins in the morning, and that evening you're at their home. The next thing you do is take her out to her friends' and relatives' homes. Do you need to explain to her that this is a home-based business?

And when you take her out, she may have some doubts, but the minute you sit down with her friends and relatives, you show the mission, what we do for families. The information is so powerful and wonderful. You show it with all your conviction. And you treat her friends and relatives with respect and kindness. Don't you think your new recruit is proud about what we do?

Now you have a real builder because she loves to go out in the field. She falls in love with the business from day one. And when she recruits somebody, she wants to go to people's homes. The minute she gets licensed, she can't wait to go out to people's homes. She can't wait to take her teammates to people's homes.

"I'd rather recruit 2 people and do it right than recruit 10 people and do it wrong. I'd rather recruit 2 people and build people who trust me than recruit 10 people who don't trust me, don't know me, and don't want to work with me seriously."

WORKING WITH YOUR SPOUSE

Having my wife involved in the business was a tough decision. One part of me knew that she could help me tremendously. The other part of me wanted to keep her at a distance.

Her involvement was sometimes challenging. One day during a BMP, my wife took over, feeling that I was just dancing around. I should go straight to the point and close it, she thought.

And every time I made a mistake, she would point it out. I did not enjoy that part much. We had so many differences about how to do the business. Moreover, her presence in the business created pressure. Sometimes I wished she was not involved. That way I'd have less expectation to succeed.

But I needed her. When I was down, trapped, or had no place to go, she always supported me. She came up with a lot of contacts for me. In fact, half of my organization comes from her.

"The best recruit is right in front of you, your spouse."

When I traveled, my wife managed the staff and the team. And of course, she took care of the family. With her help, I had more time to focus on building. I would never be able to be what I am today without her.

I am glad I asked for her support early on. Although it was difficult, I felt it was the right thing to do. I wanted to win, I knew that I would win, and I wanted her to play an essential part of it.

I saw that in some families where the spouse was not involved in the business, by the time they became successful, one spouse felt guilty while the other was resentful. Their success did not bring them happiness.

Building Together

One day, I heard a woman complain that her husband would never go with her shopping. He fired back that she would never join him when he went camping. When his wife got together with her friends, he did not want to be around. And vice versa, she would do something else when he gathered with his friends.

It happens to many families. Some think it's normal. That's the way many couples are. But that's also how people separate by degree. They're too close to pay attention to each others' interests. I got that wake up call when I joined this business. My wife was not against me doing this business. It's just that she wasn't so interested. "That's your business," she'd say. "You can do what you want."

I made a consistent effort to change that. I always asked my wife to be involved in what I do, and I also realized that I must be interested and participate in what she does.

As for the discomfort of working together, I realized the business is just a mirror of our marriage. It's not the business that was the problem. It was our relationship. We had to learn to grow together. After all, it's our future.

LISTEN CAREFULLY

When you listen

the 1st time,

you may like it.

When you listen

the 2nd time,

you understand it.

When you listen

the 3rd time,

you feel it.

When you listen

the 4th time,

you memorize it.

When you listen

the 5th time,

you apply it.

BE A CONFIDENT LEADER, NOT A CONFUSED SQUANDERER

LEADING	SQUANDERING
▶ BPM/BMP with conviction	▶ Doing a presentation
▶ Show Vision and Mission	▶ A part-time business
▶ "We're looking for serious, committed, hardworking individuals."	▶ "We will accommodate you and work with you whenever you're available."
▶ "I'll see you at 7pm with your spouse at your home."	▶ "May I come to your house tonight?"
▶ "We are going to fill out the license now, and you bring back the paperwork at 6pm tomorrow."	▶ "Here's the licensing paperwork. Go home and fill it out."
▶ "We expect you to be licensed in 3 months and become a MD in 6 months."	▶ "Can you finish licensing in 3 months and become a MD in 6 months?"

▶ "Let's work together and answer all the questions as I go through the Prospect List process."

▶ "Think of people who may join you and write their names down."

▶ Definite

▶ Iffy

▶ Clear, concise

▶ Confused, ambiguous

▶ Confident

▶ Worried about losing the recruit

▶ Tell them all the challenges of starting up the business.

▶ Keep telling them how great this business is and convincing them that it will be worth their time.

▶ Show them every step they need to do and every step you you are going to do with them.

▶ No schedule for them. No schedule for you with them.

▶ Show them the next step.

▶ "I'll see you next week."

▶ Make things happen and expect results.

▶ "Please try your best."

MD CLUB

The
Big Push

MD CLUB 3-3-30

"The building block of the system"

In the past, building was difficult and slow. The builder had to carve stone and chop down trees, then put it together to build walls, houses, and other structures. Unfortunately, most of the stones and wood were not in the same shape. Thus, it required a lot of work to fit them all together.

Then came the invention of the brick, the simple building block. Since they are all the same size, assembly took a fraction of the time of someone using odd-sized materials.

MD Club 3-3-30: The Building Block Of The System Flow

To start, the new trainee follows the trainer to build 3-3-30. With the trainer's help, he will recruit 3 direct and observe 3 PFS sales in 30 days.

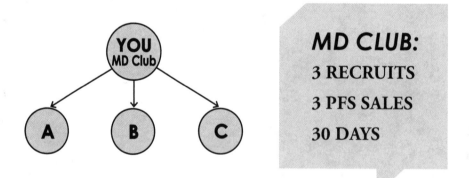

Now A, B, and C also become new trainees and run to become MD Club 3-3-30.

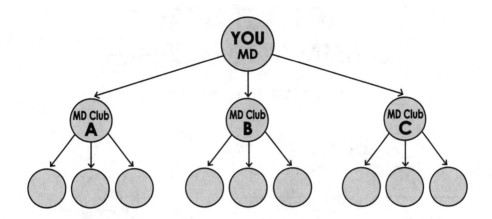

Build 3 MD Club / Build Your Way to Become MD

You become MD Club, then A, B, and C duplicate to become MD Clubs, and so on. Everyone does the same. Because of this simple duplication, you can become MD, and soon, A, B, and C can also become MDs.

It's like laying one brick at a time, and soon you will build a great wall. Behold! Through the MD Club system, we have broken the code to building a large organization.

"Building a big organization just got easier."

THE FAST START SPINNING MACHINE

"How fast can you spin?"

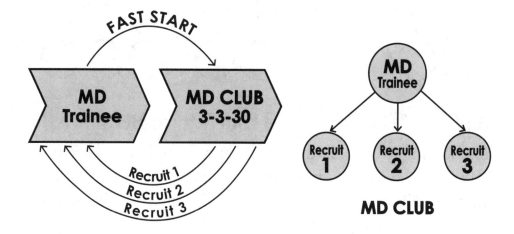

MD CLUB

When you fast start, you spin the Trainee/MD Club machine. When you spin the first cycle, you get 3 new recruits and 3 sales in 30 days. When you spin the second cycle with Recruit 1, you get another 3-3-30. When you spin two more cycles,

SPEED DUPLICATION:

The fast start spinning machine solves one of the most critical problems in building: speed duplication. Since the 3-3-30 is so simple and clear to understand, we can overcome the slow start problem, which often resulted in hesitation, doubt, fear, and failure.

you get Recruit 2 and Recruit 3 to become new MD Clubs. Every time you spin—every time you Fast Start—more recruits and more PFS sales come out.

The faster the spin—the faster the Fast Start—the faster new MD Clubs are built.

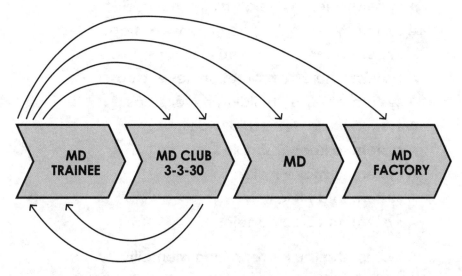

The Fast Start system works beautifully when the duplication of 3-3-30 becomes the simple focus of the organization. Everyone knows that either they have to become MD Club or they have to help someone become MD Club. Thus, we simplify, unify, and begin to multiply.

"3-3-30 opens the floodgates to fast start."

3-3-30

A system whereby recruiting never stops.

A system whereby sales never stops.

A system whereby field training never stops.

A system whereby duplication never stops.

A system whereby cash flow never stops.

A system whereby promotion never stops.

A system whereby building never stops.

A system to go deep and wide.

A system to keep it simple.

A system to make it clear.

A system to do it fast.

A system that is so doable.

A system that builds recruiting mentality.

A system to fast start a new recruit immediately.

A system to train the meeting mentality.

A system to build teamwork from the beginning.

A system that trains the trainee.

A system that builds the trainer.

A system that mobilizes everyone out to the field.

A system that builds strong replacement legs.

A system that builds a strong baseshop.

A system that builds a big hierarchy.

3-3-30 is our MD Club.

3-3-30 is our Building Block.

"Focus on 3-3-30. Your dreams can come true."

FOCUS ON YOUR FIRST 3

"The Big Push"

The purpose of MD Club is to make a big push to become MD.

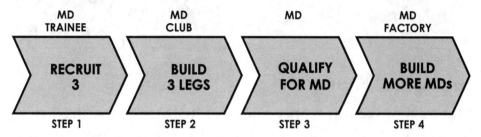

As you can see, the system is quite simple.

Step 1

When you start, you recruit 3.

Step 2

At the MD Club level, you duplicate that process with these 3 recruits to build them into 3 legs (L1, L2, L3: Leg 1, Leg 2, Leg 3).

Step 3

You qualify for MD.

Step 4

You build more MDs.

If you look at this MD Factory chart, the whole system depends on building MD Club members.

Thus, MD Club is the building block of the system. You must qualify for MD Club and build more MD Club members.

You must recruit 3, and help those 3 qualify for MD Club, and continue the duplication process.

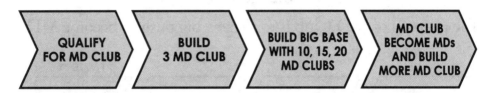

Recruit 3 Mentality

Once a new team member finds her first 3 recruits, there will be no stopping her to recruit more. Most importantly, during the initial stages when she recruits 3, she must learn how to recruit these first 3 people—PPL, BMP, drop by, follow up. She has to go through a large number of people. Thus, she gains experience and confidence to become a good recruiter.

Duplication: L1, L2, L3

This mentality must be duplicated to build 3 legs, the foundation for a solid base.

If a person qualifies for MD Club but fails to help her team members qualify for MD Club, the system won't work.

Also, the MD must overlap leadership with her trainers and make sure everyone in the base qualifies for MD Club.

FORMULA FOR SUCCESS:
$B = MDc^n$

"The formula that will change the world of building."

You get 3. Then tell these 3 to get 3. And tell these 9 to get 3. And tell these 27 to get 3. And so on…

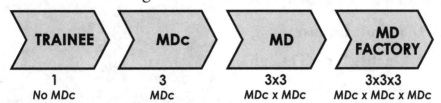

TRAINEE	MDc	MD	MD FACTORY
1	3	3x3	3x3x3
No MDc	MDc	MDc x MDc	MDc x MDc x MDc

$B = MDc^n$

Building = MDc x MDc x MDc x MDc x MDc …

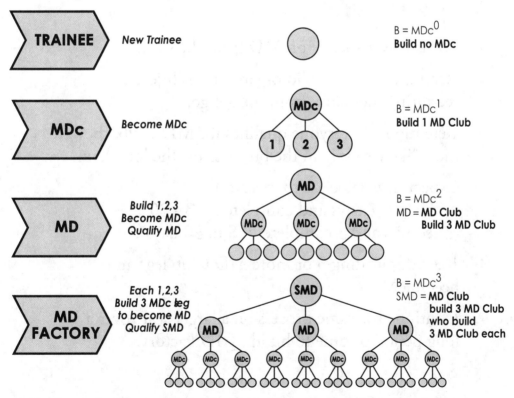

This formula focuses on MD Club. If both the builder and the team member, the trainer and the trainee, follow it, we have a clear and simple focus to build. Building and duplication become easy.

THE MD CLUB SYSTEM

"The Simple System to Build MDs"

SIMPLE PROCESS:	SIMPLE RECOGNITION:
1. Submit License	1. Obtain License
2. Qualify for MD Club	2. MD Club Shirt
3. Run for MD	3. MD Jacket

Why MD Club:

▶ Focus new associate on MD from the start.

▶ Recruit to build a solid organization. Inject a recruiting mentality from the get go.

▶ Retention. If everyone qualifies for MD Club, they are more likely to stay in the business for the long haul.

▶ Expect new associate to recruit 3 in the first 7 days and complete 3 - 3 - 30 (3 recruits and 3 complete PFS in 30 days).

▶ Keep duplicating 3 or more MD Club legs and become MD.

▶ Continue the same process on a larger scale over a long period of time to build a MD Factory.

THE MD CLUB MEETING AFTER THE MEETING

"It's easier to work with the committed."

Create a culture of focusing on MDs in the baseshop at the early stages. Identify the "want to do" versus the "one who really does it." MD Clubs are our future MDs.

Monitor:

▶ MD Checklist

▶ Organization chart

▶ Activities and results (minimum 3 points a week; a sale or recruit equals one point)

▶ Activities to be scheduled and results in the next 7 days

▶ Deadlines for licensing and MD promotion

Motivate:

▶ Welcome new qualifiers.

▶ Recognize their goals and their dreams.

▶ Build relationships among club members.

▶ Recognize achievers, big and small.

Train:

▶ Train skills and wills of the MDs-to-be.

▶ Involve club members in the business: set up, parking, meeting, convention, training, compliance, etc.

▶ Build up their presentation skills, their leadership skills, and their confidence.

Compete:

▶ Foster an environment of competition.

▶ People tend to rise to the level of their group. They believe, "If he can do it and she can do it, then I can do it."

▶ Competition eliminates fear.

Systematize:

▶ Building a baseshop, building new MDs, becomes part of a system. Young MDs can work with other MDs to build, reducing the fear of those who have small baseshops.

▶ More strength and faster speed are necessary to build MDs.

▶ MD Club members encourage and help each other to become MD.

MD CLUB MEMBERS MUST KNOW HOW TO DO BMP

*"A MD Club member is not a non-MD.
They're a MD in the making."*

MD Club Members Must Become MD Club Trainers

▶ Follow MD to the field.

▶ Practice and master the presentation.

▶ Organize and support the Home BPM.

▶ Do BMP. Take new recruits out to the field.

▶ Duplicate and build new MD Club members.

> *Once the MD Club member becomes a trainer, she can take people people out in the field and duplicate herself.*

BECOMING A MD JUST GOT EASIER

Vision Of Promotion

Which one looks more simple?

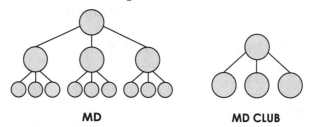

Telling them to become MD appears to be more difficult than telling them to build MD Club and their people to run for MD Club.

Power Of The MD Club

Build wide and deep. In reality, you may have to go wider and deeper to find a MD Club.

Which Organization Do You Prefer?

Both are great legs.

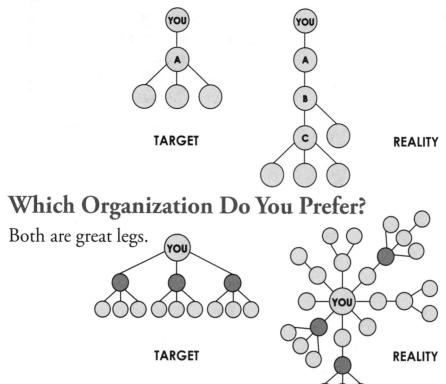

FAST START

"It is critical to have a strong start."

You Need To Fast Start A New Recruit Within 48 Hours

It's easier to strike while the iron is still hot. When he's excited, he's willing to start right away. But his enthusiasm can fade away quickly, especially when he begins to face some negativity or rejection.

Procrastination Is A Part Of Human Nature

Whenever possible, most people tend to wait it out and see what happens before doing anything. A common response is: "Once I know it, then I will do it." Thus, most of them opt to get licensed before they do anything. They'd rather learn by studying rather than learn by doing.

As a result, many fired up recruits quickly lose interest, and fear begins to set in. Licensing becomes a boring, tedious process. Most end up not getting licensed, or if they ever do, it drags on a long time. Worse, when they get licensed, they have no team and nobody to sell to. They become lonely licensed agents.

> *If people have a choice between challenging and easy, they always gravitate toward the easy way out.*

Fast Start To Spark An Explosion

If we can get them to go out with a trainer to recruit a few people, they'll explode with renewed enthusiasm. The chances of retention and of finishing licensing will be a lot higher. Help them qualify for MD Club by recruiting 3 and completing 3 PFS, and you'll have a winner.

> *FAST START THE NEW RECRUIT TO MD CLUB*
>
> **A new recruit who starts fast tends to duplicate a fast start to his team. A recruit who starts slow tends to duplicate failure to his team.**

"It's hard to ask someone to fast start if you yourself move like a snail."

BUILDERS' SUCCESS ORDERS

▶ Join - Own - Share

▶ 10 K / month per license

▶ 30 licenses in the base

CAN YOU WALK AND CHEW GUM AT THE SAME TIME?

What would you prefer to do?

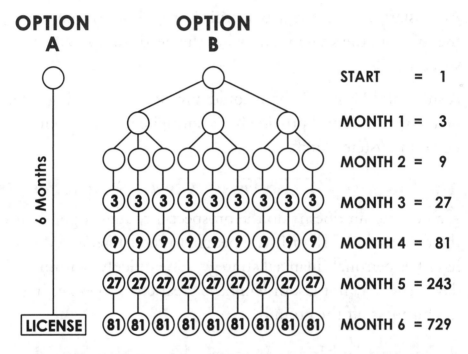

OPTION A

OPTION B

6 Months

LICENSE

START = 1

MONTH 1 = 3

MONTH 2 = 9

MONTH 3 = 27

MONTH 4 = 81

MONTH 5 = 243

MONTH 6 = 729

Spend 6 months just to study and get licensed.

Assuming you recruit just 3 people and help others recruit 3 who recruit 3 per month, in 6 months, you'll have 729 people. At the same time, you study and get licensed.

Which one would you rather have?

| LICENSE + 0 TEAM | vs. | LICENSE + 729 PEOPLE |

| NO WHERE TO GO | vs. | PLENTY OF PLACES TO GO |

"Can you recruit and get licensed at the same time?"

UPSTART SCHOOL

*"If you don't have a fast start,
you will have a slow start,
or you won't start at all."*

At Upstart School, the new recruit learns about the company, the mission, the system, and what she needs to do to become successful.

A successful Upstart School could advance the building career of a new recruit and provide her a springboard to become a powerful system builder.

The Purpose Of The Upstart Is To Retain People

If a new recruit doesn't do the prospect list, doesn't go out to the field to do BMP or invite people to the BPM, and doesn't have her personal financial strategy done quickly (within 7 days), she may not last or will have great challenges getting her business off the ground.

A Recruit Is Not A Recruit Until She Has A Recruit

With a prospect list, the trainer takes the new recruit out to do BMP/BPM, and she may recruit someone. Once she has a recruit under her, she certainly will be excited.

A Recruit Is Not A Crusader Until She Believes In Our Mission

With the training on our mission, the new recruit understands more about what we can do for the consumer and develops belief in our crusade.

A Recruit Is Not A Potential Builder Until She Follows The System

By doing the PPL, BMP/BPM, and PFS, the recruit begins to systematize, becomes coachable, and follows the system.

ADVANCED PROGRAM

In concert with Upstart School, many offices run the Advanced Program to train future trainers.

Since there is product training, attendees of the program must have already submitted their licensing. They also need to get licensed fast, so they can go out and practice what they learn.

The Advanced Program:

1. PROVIDES PROPER TIME TO TRAIN: There are subjects that require more time than the normal BPM training hour. The Advanced Program would provide that time.

2. ALLOWS MORE FOCUSED TRAINING:
In Advanced School, no time is spent on recognition and other BPM protocol.

3. GIVES MORE CONFIDENCE TO TEAM MEMBERS:
Knowledge of our concepts and products will help them understand what we do better.

4. INCREASES NUMBER OF PEOPLE WHO GET LICENSED FASTER:
The extra training helps team members pass their licensing exams.

5. THE CRUSADE-BUILDING MACHINE:
Consistent training prepares team members to offer better service for the client.

MD

The

Baseshop Building

Machine

MD: THE BASE

"The building machine."

The real focus of the system is the MD and how many MDs you are going to build. MD is the outlet of our distribution system. It's the symbol of success, the rite of passage of a system builder. Achieving the MD position is one step away from a part-timer going full time.

MD Club 3-3-30 is the first test to find out if the new trainee is the right material for MD. Thus, if the MD Club member is serious, he will build 3 MD Club legs to become MD. He demonstrates the ability to duplicate a new trainee to become MD. It shows that he can prospect, drop by, contact, field train, do presentation, recruit, sell, fast start, and duplicate people.

A MD is not a MD until he has a MD.

Building steps: You become MD, then build a MD under you.

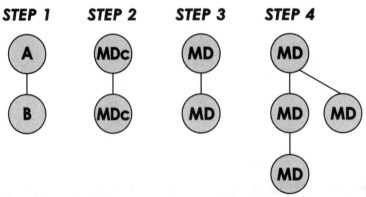

Once you can build and duplicate MDs, you are ready to run the system.

The Baseshop

The baseshop is your business. Just like a chef who owns his restaurant or the franchisee who owns his store, the MD must take charge and build his baseshop. He should have an office and staff to help him with underwriting and administration. MD is not just a new promotion. It's the pride of entrepreneurship.

"MD is the beginning of a great business,
the start of the duplication machine."

MD Baseshop Focus

Many people start the business on a part-time, flexible basis. They don't recognize the real business side of the baseshop and thus face unnecessary failures. Just like with any business, the MD must monitor the ins and outs of his operation.

1. BMP:

▶ How many trainees/trainers out in the field every night? What are their results?

▶ Make sure to match up to maximize the number of BMPs.

2. BPM:

▶ How many new guests come for the presentation?

▶ How many teammates come to the meeting?

3. MONITOR THE HOT LIST

▶ Who needs to fast start 3-3-30?

▶ Who does 5-5-30?

▶ Who does 10-10-30?

▶ Who's running for MD?

▶ What's the cash flow of your licensed agents?

4. LOCAL AND BIG EVENT

▶ How many people will be at these events? With spouses?

▶ How many people achieve promotions and awards?

5. LEADING BY EXAMPLE: MOST IMPORTANT OF ALL, YOU ARE THE KEY

▶ How many personal and field training recruits do you have?

▶ How many personal and field training sales do you do?

▶ Who are you going to build to become new MD Club trainers this month?

▶ What's your cash flow?

"Everything in the base depends 100% on you."

KNOW EXACTLY HOW TO FOCUS

The Baseshop Monitor Flow

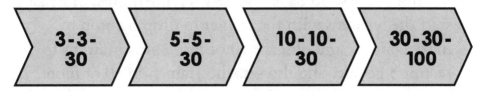

3-3-30 | 5-5-30 | 10-10-30 | 30-30-100

The Baseshop BPM Flow

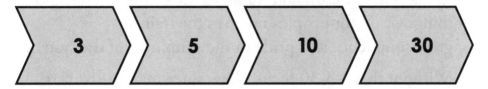

3 | 5 | 10 | 30

The number of people to the meeting twice a week.

"It's so simple. It's incredibly powerful!"

THE NEW FOCUS:
3-3-30 for the New Recruit
5-5-30 for the Trainer
10-10-30 for the MD
30-30-100 for a MD Factory

Focus To Win
The New Recruit: 3-3-30

▶ Within the first 30 days, the new recruit/trainee must fast start the business with the trainer to drop by, stop by, make contact, and observe 10 or more presentations to recruit 3 people. She also sees the Trainer do 10 or more presentations to make 3 PFS/sales. The purpose of 3-3-30 is to give the new trainee enough training and experience so that she can learn and duplicate. It also shows the good things we do for people and gives the trainee great confidence and pride in the simplicity of the system.

▶ Without this 3-3-30 focus, the trainee may let the first 30 days pass by without understanding the fundamentals of our business.

The Trainer: 5-5-30

▶ After completing 3-3-30, the trainee must become the Trainer. 5-5-30 is the number that she must always focus on.

▶ She must continue to make personal recruits and sales while beginning to field train her people to master the skills of field work.

▶ She begins to make some good part-time income.

▶ She builds discipline and winning habits to manage activities and focus on results.

▶ She prepares to become MD.

The MD: 10-10-30

▶ Overlaps to build new 3-3-30 legs and constantly fast starts new team members.

- ▶ Masters duplication.
- ▶ Builds a strong baseshop.
- ▶ Makes good income through personal and field training sales.
- ▶ Gains control and confidence.

10-10-30 is the ultimate focus for the MD. All good things come with the builder who does 10-10-30. She is in the building phase toward a MD Factory.

MD Factory: 30 – 30 – 100

30-30-100 is the simple formula for a big baseshop. If you can develop a disciplined team with 30 people who show up at the BPM twice a week, you have a strong organization. This committed group of people will normally bring about 30 new recruits per month. Thus, 100K baseshop can be easily achieved.

By focusing on a winning habit—discipline, commitment, teamwork—you can build a team of 30 to be at the BPM twice a week and have a strong base.

30 to BPM twice a week

30 Recruits a month

100K points a month

You don't need to be talented to do it. Building a big base is no longer a secret. First, try to get 3 people to be at the BPM twice a week. This is the beginning. Next, increase to 5 people. Now you have a small team, and you become a trainer. Move on to 10 people and become MD. The day you have 30, you start a MD factory.

PREPARATION FOR THE MD BASE

"Can you maintain a strong MD Base until you become financially independent?"

Have you seen a young student excel in high school then start losing steam in college, distracted and barely able to complete his degree? He enters the real world with less enthusiasm and begins a long struggle in life.

MD Traps

Most start up businesses fail. Some struggle to survive, and only a few are successful. The MD business start up is no different. The whole reason you work hard to become MD is to prepare to be big, building hundreds or even thousands of people in the future.

The system works. Unfortunately, you must work the system and avoid the career traps.

The most common mistakes that new MDs commit are:

1. WORKING AT THE SAME PACE JUST LIKE WHEN HE WAS NOT MD. Most stay part time and show up to the office twice a week for the BPM as usual! To them, MD is just a new promotion—not a big deal, a beginning of a new business, or a life-changing moment.

2. THOSE WHO GO FULL TIME ARE NOT TRULY FULL TIME. These people stay home and claim that they're working from home. They want to build a big business in their pajamas!

3. NO OFFICE, NO EQUIPMENT, NO STAFF, NO BILLS, NO RESPONSIBILITY. What a wonderful, worry-free business!

4. GETTING OVERWHELMED BY PAPERWORK. Many MDs end up doing the same routine. They prospect, answer the phone, check email, do underwriting, and order supplies by themselves and feel worn out quite quickly.

"Doing paperwork is probably one of the biggest hidden killers of building a big business."

5. DETACH TOO EARLY FROM THE UPLINE. Newly promoted MDs pull out, wanting to run their own deal. While it's great that they step up and want to be independent, many go too far into isolation and can't handle the challenges of their team.

6. MOVING MORE INTO TEACHING AND TRAINING INSTEAD OF DOING AND LEADING BY EXAMPLE.

7. TOO FOCUSED WITH THEIR TEAM AND FAIL TO BUILD NEW LEGS. Quite often, they are trapped more by people problems rather than making things happen in the field where new recruits, new sales, and new fast starts are where the action is.

8. CASH FLOW PROBLEM. Lack of personal activity can lead to cash shortages and financial problems. It will affect their attitude and their ability to perform.

9. LACK OF SPOUSAL SUPPORT. More than ever, spousal support is so badly needed for the new MD. A house divided cannot stand. Pressure mounts when the MD tries to focus and puts more time in the business. He needs to involve his family and win their support. He can't win alone. After all, it's their family's future.

"You don't win by accident. You must be prepared and fight every day until you win the baseshop battle."

LOCAL EVENT: THE GIANT BASESHOP BUILDING MACHINE

You cannot build a big team all by yourself. You build it with big building events. The local event is our giant baseshop building machine.

1. The Magic Of Crowds

When you have thousands of MD Club qualifiers in one room, you have thousands of "Building Supermen and Super-women" all under one roof. You alone cannot motivate a MD trainee effectively. But thousands of people can.

2. Leadership By Example

Every month, the trainee is exposed to great do-it-first leaders whom she can learn from and duplicate. People tend to copy their role models. This is a fast track giant duplication program.

3. Competition

Great team builders are great competitors. A competitive environment revs up the inner drive of the trainee, racing her way to the top.

4. Bring More MD Club Qualifiers

The size of your baseshop depends on the number of MD Club qualifiers inside your base.

5. Compress Time Frames, Compress Activities

Instead of waiting for annual events, we compress the frequency of events down to every few months. Everybody has an equal opportunity to build faster with this system than with only 1 or 2 events a year.

6. Focus On Building The Base

Consistent, relentless focus on the base will ensure long-term success to a new generation of big baseshop builders.

7. Predictable

The local event is like a scanning machine that examines the growth or decline of your business. To measure the buildup of future leaders, just count how many MD Club members in your base, superbase, and superteam go to the local event.

If you have more MD Club members going to the event, your team is growing. If you have less, your team is dying. And if you have the same number of MD Club members, your team is stagnating.

THINK ABOUT IT:
What if you brought 100 MD Club qualifiers to the local event?

8. Hero-Making Machine

The local event cranks out future leaders by the thousands. It's the Olympic training for future builder athletes.

9. MD Club + Events = MD

The main purpose of these events is to build a large base with 10 to 20 MD Club members. A MD Club member who goes to the event will be inspired and make a decision to become MD.

"Success goes to those leaders who consistently bring more and more people to the local event."

A SYSTEM OF DISCIPLINE

LOS ANGELES CONVENTION, 2002

The local event is a super discipline system. It allows you to recognize who in your team is disciplined enough to stay with you in the long run. If you're in business with us long enough, you'll come to appreciate the fact that we have a system.

Everything we do here requires discipline. It takes a disciplined person to go out in the field during the evening. And it takes a super disciplined person to go to the big event.

In our business we have options: you don't have to do the business every night and you don't have to go to the big event. But then you find out by the end of the day, whether you win or lose in life, it's not because you lack talent, capital, or desire. You lack discipline. You lack the things that successful people have. Discipline is the ability to do the things you hate. And that's pretty tough. The things that you don't want to do, that's what you have to do.

Everyday there are a thousand things you don't want to do. In our business, there are a zillion things you won't want to do. Every time you pick up the phone, you don't want to do it. You see that name, and you hate it. They jacked you around ten times already. But can you discipline yourself to call the eleventh time?

UNDERSTAND THIS!

*"People see what they want to see,
hear what they want to hear!"*

For many people, when we ask them to focus on recruits, they think we don't teach them the products and how to sell.

Yet when we teach them the concepts and products, they think we want to push for sales.

And when we want them to go out in the field, they insist to learn first before trying. And when they try a few times, they already want to change the system.

Or when we ask them to go to the meeting and the event to learn, they tell us they don't have time and that there are too many meetings.

But when we ask them if they want to make money, they all say they want to make big $$$.

So many people want to learn the steps, but when the music plays, they don't want to get on the dance floor.

You must be bad before you can be good. You must be good before you can get better.

*"This business is easy to do
but hard to understand!"*

MD FACTORY

*The Hierarchy/Outlets
Building Machine*

BUILD 3 MDS

"MD Factory is the threshold of big builders."

Immediately after you become MD, you must build your first 3 MDs to create a MD Factory.

Build MDs

As a new MD, your main focus should be to quickly identify 3 potential MDs-to-be in your base. As you work relentlessly with these people and help them become MD, you develop the skills of a builder.

The common mistake of many newly promoted MDs is to learn the role of the MD. Just like the young man who moves out of his parents' house and is preoccupied with all the necessary things for the new apartment, young MDs try to set up the office, do paperwork, learn to run the baseshop, learn to run the show. These distractions may set them back or slow them down greatly.

> **Building your first MD is always the hardest. The next aren't as difficult.**

If you don't see 3 potential MDs in your base, you must go out and recruit more. Don't wait for a miracle.

MD FACTORY

"It's hard to build a big base.
But it's even harder to build a big hierarchy."

Most builders have great challenges building and maintaining a big hierarchy. That's why a lot of people cease to grow once they achieve a certain level.

1. Alignment of Success

If you grow a little backyard garden, you can do it yourself. But if you want to have a big farm, you need help. Likewise, if you want to build a big hierarchy, you need coaching. Everybody needs coaching, whether a brand new trainee, a field leader, a MD, or even a CEO. Having a good coach boosts your confidence and your team's confidence.

The Great Leader Generation (GLG) is the best coaching program for future System Builders. GLG is an attempt to provide future giant builders a breeding ground for growth, a haven from being trapped by their own small team. For you to grow, you need to align yourself with someone bigger than you. Otherwise, your team's potential will be limited by your own potential.

"It's hard to show someone how to do things
bigger than what you are doing.
It's hard to show someone how to make more money
than what you are making."

GLG members must maintain 10-10-30 every month to qualify. New MDs are coached and supported by the best builders in the industry. If you want to win, join a winning program.

2. Be Part Of A Winning Team

When you're in a team of great builders, your chances of winning increase tenfold. This is the secret to the success of our business. In the industry, there are a lot of good people, but they tend to play their lonely game. It's difficult to find any big builders in the industry, and if there are, they probably don't work together.

"Our goal is to help builders be in business for themselves but not build by themselves."

3. Builders Build Bigger Together

The network of leaders provides sideline motivation and cooperation to build long distance. It's a great way to build multiple baseshops in multiple locations. This is a perfect example of teamwork on a national level.

4. The Bigger You Are, The More Coachable You Should Be

There's no better way to demonstrate the greatness of a leader than by showing that he's also a good follower, a coachable team member.

5. How Many Leaders In Your Team Qualify For GLG?

Wouldn't you want your CEO to take care of your superstar and free up your time to go out, recruit, and build more of them?

COACHABLE VS. TEACHABLE

Ability to Follow	Ability to Learn
Follower	Student of the Business
Stumble Forward	Understand the Reason
Fire Up w/ Emotion	Justify w/ Logic
Strategic Move	Tactical Execution
Tell Them	Show Them
Order	Instruct

*"Coach them first. Teach them after.
Do it first, and you will learn."*

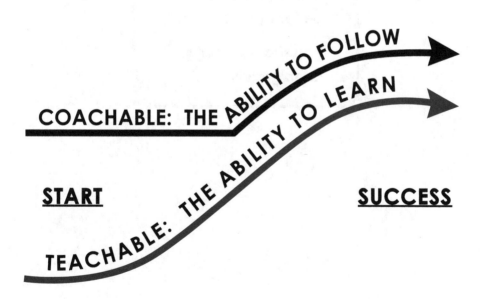

When you start, you don't know a lot. You need a ton of coachability. In the first few years, be totally coachable, follow your leader, and follow the system. Align yourself with our successful system builders.

Eventually, when people begin to learn and accumulate knowledge and experience, they think they know a lot. They become uncoachable too soon and end up making big mistakes that damage their career prematurely and unnecessarily. The minute most MDs get promoted, they do things on their own, and most struggle after that.

> *You should always be coachable.*
>
> *You should always be teachable.*
>
> *You should always keep growing.*

THE MIGHTY FORCE OF HABIT

"The individual who wants to

reach to the top in business

must appreciate the might

of the force of habit—and must

understand that practices

are what create habits.

He must be quick to

break those habits that can

break him—and hasten

to adopt those practices that

will become the habits that help

him achieve the

success he desires."

— J. PAUL GETTY

YOU ARE A PRODUCT OF YOUR ENVIRONMENT

HOUSTON CONVENTION, 2002

A lot of times you handicap yourself by limiting yourself to the standards of other builders. You do yourself a disservice.

What's the dangerous game of comparison? When people compare, do they compare themselves to the highest standard or the lowest? They often follow the lowest. Too bad some of you compare yourself to the lowest of the low.

Imagine you are in an office where people make two sales a month, and because you make four sales a month, people say, "Man, you're a hero!" Then by that standard, you're trapped.

But let's say you're in an environment where making one sale a day is normal, and thirty sales a month is the norm. The day you don't make a sale you feel bad.

A bunch of guys in my office start acting like the people around them. That's where they're dead.

You go to my office, and you always see a lot of people sitting around. This MD is in front of the computer, the next MD is in front of the computer, and you look at the MD across and he's also on the computer. So you too want to be on the computer. When you get to the office, you're dead on arrival.

You box yourself in the situation. Did you know you are what environment you're in? Whatever environment you're in, that's what you become. Every one of you dies from your own environment. Unless you change the environment. Did you know that if one guy in the office talks about the wrong product, the whole office is dead? Just one guy. Do you know that only one guy needs to have the flu to infect everybody?

If you do not understand the power of The System Flow and you are not applying it properly, the minute you go back to your office and revert to the same old mode, then you're dead. You walk in your office with the same standards, and you're totally dead.

Unless you get out of your box. Get out of the box!

MD FACTORY: A SYSTEM WHEREBY BUILDING MDS NEVER STOP

Build MDs:

CREATE A PIPELINE
MD Trainee ⇨ MD Club ⇨ MD ⇨ MD Factory

Every MD Trainee qualifies for MD Club.

Every MD Club member qualifies for MD.

Every MD works to build a MD Factory.

Build Hierarchy:

Every MD must set a goal on the number of MDs they plan to build.

TARGET SPEED:
"Double your MDs every 3 months."
– XUAN'S MD LAW

By running the MD Club/MD Factory, you can build an incredible number of MDs in just one year.

If You Have 2 MDs In January:

You can have 4 MDs by April,

8 MDs by July,

16 MDs by October,

32 MDs by the end of the year.

SYSTEM BUILDER BUSINESS MODEL

"The winning model for the 21st century."

1. Duplication
2. Mission-driven
3. Inter-independence
4. Entrepreneurship

Most people go into business without a clear picture of what they want to build. Many people are flip floppers who copy other people's models and use formulas that may not fit well with their business situation or market. By chasing after others, they get confused and often end up failing.

In our business, many teammates do not think about a business model because they do not recognize its importance. And if the blind follow the blind, where do they end up?

1. DUPLICATION: Sales, recruits, promotions… all of this is important, but by the end of each month and every year, how many MDs and System Builders that you built are the true targets. The number of MDs you duplicate that can run a successful business is what really matters.

2. MISSION-DRIVEN: Our business must be mission driven. Helping people, helping the consumer, helping our teammates become successful—that is our purpose. Helping people is not a philosophy; it's our business. Mission driven is the oxygen for endurance. A mission driven team cannot fail. A man and woman of mission will not stop.

> **LOOK AT THE SALMON.**
>
> *No matter what ocean or river they're in, no matter how long the journey, how strong the current, how tired, hurt and battered they are, each and every one of them knows their mission.*

3. INTER-INDEPENDENCE: We must be independent. That's where our strength lies. A weak person, a weak team member, always depends on someone else.

Coachable does not mean dependable or amenable. Coachability is quite often misunderstood by both team members and upline leaders, which leads to abuse and weakens the team. Coachability only works when there is the presence of integrity in the leadership and the system. Strong members and strong leaders are very coachable in established institutions, such as the church, the military, or the judicial system. Follow your upline, but don't follow blindly.

Now, if you are independent, you can work independently with other independent people from different teams. By then, you can be inter-independent. Inter-independence is very critical in our business model. It gives you, the entrepreneur, the chance to work with other downline, sideline, and upline with confidence. It helps open your mind, your market, and your expansion. It also allows you to make good decisions for your business to grow.

4. ENTREPRENEURSHIP: This is a flexible business. It gives you the chance to work part-time or full-time. It allows you to move at your own pace.

But it is a business nonetheless, and a serious one. It's not a fly-by-night operation or one of those quick-fix deals without real commitment. To succeed, you must be as disciplined as any successful businessperson. You should invest time, effort, and money into the business. Remember: More investment means more potential for return; less investment means less potential for return. Always invest and reinvest back into the business.

Every dollar you spend for office and staff, you invest into your business. Every dollar you spend for your business—on materials, education, meetings, events and traveling—you invest into your future. Every dollar you spend for your team— on awards and recognition—you invest into their future.

> *"Always duplicate new builders.*
> *Always be mission driven. Always be independent.*
> *Always be an entrepreneur."*

RECRUITING

*The secret of success
is not in your luck or talent.*

*It is in having many talented people
working with you and for you.*

*You have a chance to bring in not only
hundreds but thousands of people
working in your organization.*

*This is where ordinary people can do
extraordinary things.*

Focus on recruits.

Your dreams can come true.

RECRUITING MENTALITY

It's hard to describe something as abstract as a "mentality," no less a recruiting mentality. For the more I try to describe it, the more I deviate from the real meaning. In French, they say, "*Traduire, c'est trahir,*" which means to translate is to betray.

For example, how do you define "love"? Can you explain "a song"? Can you describe "air"? Can you show "water" to the fish? How about what it means to be "a parent"?

> **How about a "gambler's mentality"?**
> **The gambler has a gambling mentality.**
> **He is totally focused.**
> **He can sit for hours, even days, without tiredness or distraction.**
> **He puts everything he's got on the line.**
> **He's in the game.**
> **What about a recruiter's mentality?**
> **Do you have the same intensity?**

You probably never can. You can talk about it. You can hear of some experience about it. But you would never fully know it until you live through it and live with it.

Recruits Are The Lifeline Of Your Business

No recruits and your organization dies, like a body lacking air. Without recruits, there will be no BPMs, no BMPs, no meetings, no field training, no sales, no money, no promotions, no hope, no dreams, and no mission. Without recruits, you're in a state of coma.

Recruiting Is A State Of Urgency And Emergency!
"Business opportunity and a sense of urgency always go together."

YOU MUST BE EXCITED
"Either you infect them with your enthusiasm and inject them with your crusade, or they will reject and eject you."

▶ Excitement creates curiosity. Enthusiasm breeds confidence.

▶ Set yourself on fire with enthusiasm, and when people come to watch you burn, recruit them.

▶ 90% of recruiting is being excited. Nobody would listen to or follow a non-excited person.

▶ Your excitement comes from the belief in our mission of doing great things to help people and the faith that you will win.

YOU MUST BE IN A HURRY

▶ You must always be on the run.

▶ When you talk on the phone, don't sit. Stand up. Walk around. Smile.

▶ When you drop by, tell them that you only have limited time, that you must get to the next appointment soon, that you won't be there long.

▶ When you do the BPM, tell them you wish you had more time. This thing moves fast.

▶ When you talk to your team, tell them you can't wait to run.

"If you can run and smile at the same time, you understand recruiting."

You'd Better Be Running

Every morning,

a gazelle wakes up.

It knows it must run faster

than the fastest lion

or it will be killed.

Every morning,

a lion wakes up.

It knows it must outrun

the slowest gazelle

or it will starve to death.

It doesn't matter

whether you are

a lion or a gazelle:

When the sun comes up,

you'd better be running!

— AFRICAN PROVERB

THE LAW OF AVERAGES AND THE LAW OF LARGE NUMBERS

The Numbers Business

The law of averages must be observed. If you flip a coin 1 time, you may get 1 head or 1 tail. If you flip a coin 3 times, you may get all 3 heads or all 3 tails. But if you flip a coin 10 times or more, you definitely will get some heads and some tails.

Likewise, if you talk to 1 person, you may get a Yes or a No. If you talk to 3 people, you

MORE TALK = MORE RECRUITS
NO TALK = NO RECRUITS

may get all 3 Nos or all 3 Yeses. But if you talk to 10 people or more, you will get some Yeses and some Nos.

Unfortunately, many new recruits talk to 3 or 4 friends who say No to them and give up too early.

Talk To Many People Many Times

Even if you only talk to one person, talk to him many times. If you talk to him 1 time, he may say No. If you talk to him 3 or 4 times, he may still say No. But if you keep talking, he may say Yes someday.

REMEMBER: It's a numbers business. The more you talk, the more you contact, the more chances you'll have of getting a Yes.

RECRUIT: HOW OR WHY?

"If you have a big enough why, you will figure out how."

One of the most frequently asked questions in this business is: "How do I recruit?"

We have classes and training on how to do PPL, how to make contact, how to drop by, how to do a BMP, how to invite, etc. But all of these "How to" sessions don't matter much. Maybe 10%.

If you want to be successful doing something, especially recruiting, you don't need a lot of know how. You need to know why.

Recruiting Is 90% Why And Only 10% How

For example: If we decide to make a "special offer" that if anyone recruits 10 people in 30 days, we will promote them to MD. If this were the case, most people would qualify for MD in less than a month.

In fact, some of them will qualify in a few days.

So although people may not yet know how, the reason why—to become a MD—was so strong that they would go out and do it, whether they knew how or not.

Another example: Let's say we "guarantee" an income of $100,000 per year if you personally recruit 5 people each month for the next 12 months. If that were true, there would be a long line of people signing up for this job.

Why Do You Do This Business?

Write down the top 10 reasons why you do this business. Write down the things you want to accomplish so badly in your life—the reasons that will change your life and the lives of your loved ones, reasons like providing for your kids, buying your dream home, or taking your parents on a vacation of a lifetime.

One of my top 10 reasons when I joined the business was to retire my wife from her job, something I wanted to do since we got married. I was able to achieve this goal 2 years after I joined the business.

If these reasons are really important to you, you will prospect, you will recruit, you will do whatever it takes to succeed. All the Nos won't affect you much because your reason to go on is strong.

*"If the reason is strong enough,
you'll find a way."*

TOP 10 REASONS

Write down your top 10 reasons why you do this business and read them everyday—every morning when you wake up and every night before you go to sleep. Do it until you achieve your goal.

I do this business because:

1. _____

2. _____

3. _____

4. _____

5. _____

6. _____

7. _____

8. _____

9. _____

10. _____

RECRUITS SOLVE ALL PROBLEMS OF THE BUSINESS

- ▶ When you have no appointments, **RECRUIT!**
- ▶ When you have no money, **RECRUIT!**
- ▶ When you have no momentum, **RECRUIT!**
- ▶ When you are frustrated with your team, **RECRUIT!**
- ▶ When your team doesn't recruit, **RECRUIT!**
- ▶ When your team doesn't sell, **RECRUIT!**
- ▶ When your team complains, **RECRUIT!**
- ▶ When your team loses the dream, **RECRUIT!**
- ▶ When your team has no excitement, **RECRUIT!**
- ▶ When your team misses a meeting, **RECRUIT!**
- ▶ When the market drops, **RECRUIT!**
- ▶ When somebody quits, **RECRUIT!**
- ▶ When your big star disappears, **RECRUIT!**
- ▶ When you're feeling down, **RECRUIT!**
- ▶ When you think about your family, **RECRUIT!**
- ▶ When you want to help somebody, **RECRUIT!**
- ▶ When you want to be somebody, **RECRUIT!**
- ▶ When you have to be at a party, **RECRUIT!**
- ▶ When you go shopping, **RECRUIT!**
- ▶ When your car breaks down, **RECRUIT!**
- ▶ When you get a traffic ticket, **RECRUIT!**
- ▶ When you go to the dentist, **RECRUIT!**
- ▶ When you want to win, **RECRUIT!**
- ▶ When your team wants to win, **RECRUIT!**

YOU RECRUIT AND RECRUIT AND RECRUIT!!!

RECRUIT QUANTITY

"One recruit a day keeps poverty away."

Warm Market

▶ Recruit people you know well: friends, relatives, co-workers, neighbors.

▶ Your natural market helps you get started. You can quickly get your top 25 names in this market, qualify the first 5, and drop by to do BMP, or invite them to the BPM.

▶ You can recruit 3 in the first 30 days to qualify for MD Club. That is the minimum, but you should do more than that.

*"Your warm market is sometimes not that warm.
They can give you a lot of negativity,
and you tend to take it personally!"*

Lukewarm Market

▶ Recruit acquaintances and referrals: people you meet, people you come across everyday, people you do business with, your customers, the salesperson, a friend of a friend, the technician across the hall, etc.

REMEMBER: It's just the beginning. Nobody relies on just friends and family to build a business, any business, for the long term. So don't get so frozen by your warm market.

▶ You may know hundreds of these people. You can also get referrals from people you know. These people are the backbone of your prospect list. This is the market that you go to work with everyday. Add new names to the prospect list, make contact, build relation-ships, send a brochure, or drop off a book.

▶ The prospect lists of your teammates are also from the lukewarm market. With these lists, you should never run out of places to go or people to call.

"The lukewarm market is an endless source of prospects."

Cold Market

▶ You can recruit strangers by look-ing up people on a telephone list, knocking on peo-ple's doors, run-ning into people at the shopping mall, anybody. But of course, it's cold.

Please note that our system is not doing well with the cold market. So don't bank on it. It puzzles me to see people prospect the cold market while they have many people in the warm and luke-warm markets untouched!

The odds of recruiting these people are slim. Then again, you never know. I came from the cold market. The person who recruited me met me cold in a building hallway.

"The warm market can be very cold, and the cold market can sometimes be very warm."

The Market Is Ready For A Recruiting Explosion

BABY BOOMERS: There are 76 million baby boomers in the United States. Most are in their 60's. Retirement is around the corner. Many of them are dying for a solution. Many have been laid off, some several times. Many have jobs they don't like. But they don't want to be recruited. They need somebody who cares and shows them a solution. Show them your belief. Show them this is something different.

GENERATION X: Gen Xers are in their 40s and 50s. For many, the writing is on the wall. Maybe they were laid off. Maybe they have the wrong job and are looking for a way out. Most of them do not like to go to a meeting or a seminar, but they're willing to listen if you care enough to come to their place.

THE YOUNGER GENERATIONS: Most young people are smart. Many of them don't want to make the same mistakes of the past generation. A lot of young people nowadays know they want to be in business.

THE EMPLOYED: They should consider a second career.

THE UNEMPLOYED: They definitely need to check out a new career.

THE UNDEREMPLOYED: This can be the answer for them.

THE AMBITIOUS: Our opportunity will give them a chance to build a big business.

DISSATISFIED: We can show them the way out.

THE FINANCIAL INDUSTRY: They may want to be in a better team and a better company with a better system.

THE NON-FINANCIAL INDUSTRY: They should definitely look into our wonderful industry.

THE PROFESSIONAL AND THE ENTREPRENEUR: They cannot miss the best business opportunity of a lifetime.

THE DAY SHIFTER - THE NIGHT SHIFTER - THE ODD HOURS SHIFTER: They should shift to a no-shift career. They can take control of their time. The only thing they need to do is to shift to a higher gear in their life.

THE DESPERATE: This business can give them hope.

THE CONFUSED: This can be the system they can follow.

THE DREAMER AND THE MOVER AND SHAKER: They can build it big, impact tens of thousands of people, and make a difference in the world.

THE MEN AND WOMEN ON A MISSION: This is something to believe in.

THE UNRECOGNIZED AND UNAPPRECIATED: Here, they can be somebody. They can be proud and successful. They can be on top of the world.

THE EXCITED: This will fit their character.

THE SHY: They can learn to overcome their shyness and gain confidence.

THE HIGHLY EDUCATED: They won't be trapped by their degree.

THE LESS EDUCATED: They won't be handicapped by their lack of education. Here, they earn through their effort, not by their I.Q.

THE OPTIMISTIC: Here, they can help people.

THE WORRIED: They can build something solid and secure.

THE RISK TAKER: How big can they build?

THE TIMID: We will be there for them.

THE STRONG: This will test their strength and leadership ability.

THE WEAK: Here, we work together as a team.

THE MARRIED: They should do this for their family.

SINGLES: They have plenty of time.

SALESPEOPLE: Can they sell the business? Can they sell something bigger than just products and services?

PEOPLE AFRAID OF SELLING: We just share information.

PEOPLE WHO LIKE CHANGE: This could be the best change they could make.

PEOPLE WHO DON'T LIKE CHANGE: Life will change them anyway. May as well do it now.

THE RICH: They could set a good example and share what they know.

THE POOR: It's time they made some real money.

THE MIDDLE AMERICAN: They should make a difference for others, for their family, and for their own life.

"Let's recruit the world!"

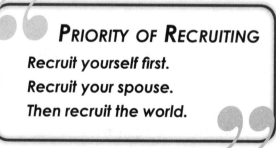

PRIORITY OF RECRUITING
Recruit yourself first.
Recruit your spouse.
Then recruit the world.

RECRUIT THE QUALITY MARKET

RECRUIT THE 7 POINTERS:

1. **Over 25 years old**
2. **Married**
3. **Children**
4. **Income**
5. **Homeowner**
6. **Ambitious**
7. **Dissatisfied**

Your chances of growing a successful business are better with "quality" people because people know people like themselves.

If They're Young, They Will Recruit Young People

People who are less than 25 years old are likely still in school or just finished with college. They have a different focus. Education is probably their first priority, as are finding a job and starting up their life. Not to mention they probably have a relationship and are preparing for marriage.

Most young recruits come and go. They normally get very excited and bring in a lot of people. But later on, they can't sell, most of their market is young, they don't have money, and they don't have urgent needs. Many end up never finishing licensing either.

If They're Too Old, They Are Often Too Reserved

They're not easily excited like the young people. They're very conservative. Many have been shafted by their boss or their co-workers.

When they go out to recruit their friends and relatives, it's the most difficult market to break into. Most people tell them it's too late, and they probably agree with them.

If They're In The Poor Market, They Will Recruit People From The Poor Market

Poor people are often too busy making ends meet. Many lack confidence. Most of them have no money. They can barely survive. How can they think about saving or investing?

If They're Too Rich, They May Not Need Our Opportunity

If they are already financially independent, they may be too comfortable and satisfied to start a new career.

Look For The Qualified Market

People who are over 25, married with kids, and who own a home have a lot of responsibility. They have needs to protect their family, to save for their children's education, and to invest long term for their retirement, and they may have some disposable income to do it. They know people like them too. They want to make money, but they begin to face reality. Their job won't help them achieve security or prosperity. And they have multiple sources motivation: their spouse, their kids, their parents, their hope to be somebody.

THE 8TH POINT: COACHABLE

"Coachability: The true quality factor."

For many years, whenever I recruited people, I always wanted to look for the quality recruit. I understood that I must recruit a lot of people, that I shouldn't prejudge people, and that my superstar could be anybody. "As long as I keep recruiting tons of people," I told myself, "I would find somebody who wants it as bad as I do." And I did find quite a few.

THE 7 POINTERS

1. 25+ years old
2. Married
3. Children
4. Homeowner
5. Income
6. Ambitious
7. Dissatisfied

After recruiting thousands, I found that the first 5 points were important but not that important, because I recruited a lot of people who had the first 5 points, the people in the "good market," but they still quit the business as fast as the ones who had fewer points.

Then I discovered that the 6th point is more important than the first 5 because it doesn't matter whether they're in the "right market". If they're not ambitious, there's not much we can do for them. If they are not hungry, if they have no desire, if they do not want to be big, they won't do anything.

Later I discovered another surprise. There are many people in the "right market" who have ambitions but still fail in the business. It's the 7th point—dissatisfied—which is key, I thought, because it doesn't matter if they are ambitious or if they want to be successful. If they're already happy with their current situation, if they're content with their job and they have good income, they won't do anything either.

Unless their back is against the wall, unless they're so unhappy about their situation, unless they're sick and tired of being sick and tired, unless they have a high level of frustration... they won't do anything. Ever since I had that realization, I didn't care about any other qualities. I just looked for the ambitious and the dissatisfied. So with all my effort, I paid special attention to these people.

But even these people still quit! I was miserable! How can these people—who have the right qualities, who say they want it bad, who say they hate their jobs—how can so many of them fail?

Finally, I got a rude awakening. These people were uncoachable. Again, it didn't matter that they had all the qualities of the "right" person. If they're not coachable, they quit just as fast as any other.

Many of these men and women look like a million bucks. They dress right. They say the right things. But they're too impressed with themselves. The minute they start the business, they question, they demand, but they don't want to listen.

They do things their way. They come and go as they please. They seem to be busy or have something more important happening all the time. But they keep telling me they want it bad! They give me hope one day and disappointment the next. They put me through an emotional roller coaster.

Ultimately, I discovered the true factor of success. In just about every successful builder whom I have had a chance to work with, I found that each one was very coachable. Many of them don't even have 2 or 3 points. At first glance, they may look like they're from the wrong market. They look very simple, very average, but deep down they're hungry, they're dissatisfied, they're willing to listen, to learn, and to try. And that makes all the difference.

The 8th Point

Now, the first quality I look for is point number 8. Without coachability, the whole system collapses. In a system, you must follow what's necessary to make the system work.

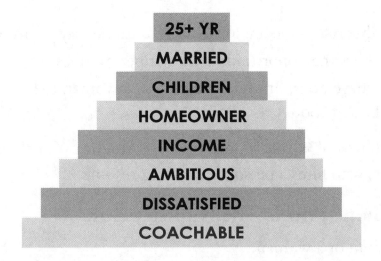

"Coachability is the #1 quality of a system builder."

RECRUIT QUANTITY TO GET QUALITY

"If you judge people,
there is no time to love them."

— MOTHER THERESA

If you prejudge people, you may not take the time to get to know them.

Who you should recruit, who you should work with, is always the big question in our business. However, there are 3 problems to finding the right person.

▶ **Problem #1:** You are not a fortune teller. You cannot predict who will be the right person for the business.

▶ **Problem #2:** You are not God. You cannot say, "This person deserves the opportunity and that person doesn't."
You have no right to deny a man or a woman the chance to be somebody.

▶ **Problem #3:** This is not corporate America. You are not a boss who hires a person based on a resume.

So Then Who Is The Right Person?

▶ A man or a woman?

▶ The one with the degrees?

▶ The one with high test scores?

▶ What kind of background?

▶ What kind of talent?

▶ What kind of appearance?

It Is Impossible To Prejudge A Winner By His Or Her Appearance Or Background

You cannot judge a book by its cover. There is no way you can tell if a person can make it until you give them a chance. In fact, almost all predictions turn out to be wrong.

There is no such thing as a small guy or a big shot. You never know. A lot of simple-looking people turn out to be superstars, while a lot of big shots turn out to be big flops.

By the way, what's a "quality" person anyway? A quality person should be judged by their work ethic, their character, the way they treat others, and the way they live their life—not by their degrees, wealth, looks, or background.

Although in earlier chapters we do talk about looking for the 7 pointers—25+ years, married, kids, income, home, ambitious, dissatisfied—this suggestion has little basis in finding winners. It just describes a defined market.

You Must Recruit Quantity To Get Quality

From a large number of people, the winners will rise up. That's why you must recruit a lot of people. You have better odds of finding good builders among 100 recruits than among 10.

MORE RECRUITS = MORE WINNERS
LESS RECRUITS = LESS WINNERS
NO RECRUITS = NO WINNERS

Don't Pick A Winner Too Early

Some people recruit a person with 6 or 7 points and think they found a superstar. Don't celebrate too soon. It's impossible to know. In fact, someone who comes in and explodes right away may not last, while somebody else who struggles in the early years can turn out to be the toughest and the strongest in the long run.

> *"This is a business of desire, discipline, character, and endurance. This is a test of will, not skill. Anybody can be a winner."*

RECRUIT THE LOW HANGING FRUIT

"Two men with the same basket went to an apple farm. The first picked the apples within his reach and moved fast from one tree to the next. The other was more choosy. He looked for the right size, color, and look. He even found a ladder to climb up to pick the ones up high. After a while the first one had his basket full, while the second one was still barely getting a few apples."

WHAT IF WE RECRUIT TOO MANY PEOPLE?

When I first came to the US, I saw so many cars.

The US auto industry, I read, sells 16 million new cars every year. At that rate, I figured out that they will soon sell an automobile to every man, woman, and child in this country. The market would be saturated in no more than a few years. Well, that never happened, and the auto industry keeps on selling.

I was also worried for the housing industry. I saw too many new homes being built and too many people getting into real estate. Eventually, there would be too many vacant homes and too many agents, I thought.

When I first started the business, I calculated that if everyone just recruits 3, and those 3 recruit 3, and so on, it would only be a few months before we would recruit the entire country. Well, that didn't happen either, because just as every car won't last forever and every real estate agent won't stick around, so it is with our recruits. Over the last 26 years in the business, we keep recruiting, we keep working hard, and yet our efforts feel like only a drop in the bucket.

RECRUIT UP, NOT DOWN

"It's easier to recruit down."

Most people tend to recruit "down". For example, you recruit a manager, the manager recruits the engineer, the engineer recruits the technician, the technician recruits the production line worker, and finally the production line worker recruits the janitor.

However, things that look easy may not turn out to be that easy. Once you head into the wrong market, it's hard to build further. If that's so, then what's left for you to recruit?

The good news is that you have plenty of quality market. There are a lot of people in the quality market out there looking for help and for an opportunity. In many cases, I found it is sometimes easier to recruit the person who makes $100K a year than it is to recruit the one who makes $30K. The former tends to have a stronger desire and wants to make more money, while the latter tends to settle, accepts things the way they are, and has no plan to make a change.

Also, people who seem to be in the wrong market may not be the wrong recruit after all. There are a lot of successful builders who come from the young, single market. There are both people from very poor backgrounds as well as people from very wealthy backgrounds who thrive in our business.

MOVE LIKE WATER

*"The army's disposition of force is like water.
Water configures its flow in accord with the terrain.
Water has no constant shape."*

-SUN TZU

You know why we call it The System Flow? Because it flows. Anything that works so hard won't flow.

Keep flowing. Move like water. Water doesn't try so hard, but it flows. When water hits a rock, it avoids the rock and goes around it. Water sees the high land and never tries to climb it. Water takes the low road. That's how water flows.

This is also how you do the business. You always got to keep moving. If people don't join, move on. If people don't buy, move on. If people don't want to build, move on.

Don't hit your head against the wall trying to convince the rock to buy, to join, or to do something it doesn't want to do. Just move on.

Keep It Simple

"Flow, don't form."

FLOW	FORM
Simplify	Complicate
Unify	Divide
Multiply	Fragment

RECRUITING MINDSET

"Believe that life is worth living and your belief will help create the fact."
— WILLIAM JAMES

▶ *"This is a breakthrough!"*

▶ *"I'm so lucky!"*

▶ *"I believe in this business!"*

▶ *"This is my way out!"*

▶ *"This is my wake-up call!"*

▶ *"I can do it!"*

▶ *"This is the time!"*

▶ *"It's proven!"*

▶ *"What an incredible system!"*

▶ *"What a powerful concept!"*

▶ *"What a historic moment!"*

▶ *"This is the future!"*

*"Don't recruit people.
Show them your belief."*

THE EMOTIONAL CONNECTION

"People react to emotion."

Logic Or Emotion?

Whenever we make decisions, we tend to calculate the pros and cons. We use our logic to evaluate the calories in a meal, the capacity of a computer, the features of a car. We compare shoes, shirts, and pants by feeling the material, looking at the color, and finding the right size. It seems we're very logical.

But in fact, most of the time, we are not so logical. When we go shopping, we intend to buy a shirt but end up with a suit. We stick to a diet for the whole day but end up eating a big dessert. We intend to buy a Toyota but drive home with a Lexus. We buy all sorts of things we never use, like expensive shoes that are rarely worn or car options that are never used.

That's why the salesperson at the department store says, "You look so good in that suit. This color makes you look so much younger!" The salesperson's not going to tell you, "This suit costs $1,000!"

> **Most of us react with our feelings and emotions more often than with our logic. Hey, we're human.**

When we do this business, we must always understand the mighty force of emotion. When we get connected to or affected by something, we will make decisions about it. Our job is to get the client involved and to take the issue that is important to them seriously. Our job also is to make them understand these issues, so that they can make the right decision for their life.

Emotion Creates Motion

"When we get so disappointed about something,
we will quit doing it.

When we get so excited about something,
we will jump into it.

When we care so much about something,
we will take care of it."

When you want your prospect, your client or your team member to do something, don't talk logic. Get into their heart. Connect with their emotions.

Logically, most people would recruit 1 person a month. But when they're on fire, they recruit 10 people a week.

Move Them With Emotion But Back It Up With Logic

When you sell to people, sell them the responsibility of taking care of their family and the possibility of building wealth for their family's future. At the same time, back it up with facts, figures, and track records. Otherwise, they may make a decision to buy but will cancel when they think it over! On the other hand, you may show the client all the performance results, the investment options, and the tax advantages, yet never find out what's most important to them. People don't buy a product. They buy the thing that improves their life. Therefore, make sure that the products fit their needs and are affordable.

Likewise, when you recruit people, you can sell the dream of being somebody and being a crusader. But you must back it up with local examples of success, people who are living their dream. You must also show them a system that can help them

LOGIC		EMOTION
Don't want to recruit	*but*	Want to be Marketing Director
Don't want to sell	*but*	Want to be on a mission
Don't want to do PPL	*but*	Want to help people they know
Don't want a second career	*but*	Want to be financially independent
Don't want to join	*but*	Want to invest their time
Don't want to buy	*but*	Want to take care of their family
Don't want a boss	*but*	Want to follow a leader
Don't want to go to the meeting	*but*	Want to experience a life-changing event
Don't want to make money on friends	*but*	Want friends to be successful in business
Don't want to sell to relatives	*but*	Has the responsibility to share what they know
Don't do things for themselves	*but*	Would do it for the team's pride
Don't want to push anyone	*but*	Want them to win
Don't want a shirt	*but*	Want to be recognized
Don't want a system	*but*	Want to be a giant builder

"Get into what's important to them emotionally."

do it, a training program that's proven to work. They need to know all of the great products and solutions we have to help people. Otherwise, their logical mind, or a negative colleague, will explain how impossible it will be for them to succeed.

If you want your team to move, find out their hot buttons. That's why you should ask your team to write down their top 10 reasons why they do this business. So when they're down, you remind them of those things.

I do not know many people dying to get a new house, a new car, or a new title. But I know a lot of people who want to be special, who want to be recognized, and who want to be proud of themselves and make their family proud of them.

You must know your people. You must have true relationships with your people in order for you to help them.

RECRUITING VISION

Recruiting and Vision are two sides of the same coin. Recruiting is:

▶ Having the Vision

▶ Sharing the Vision

If you see it, then you can share what you see. Thus, a team member who doesn't recruit or who slows down on recruits may not have a positive vision of the business or their future.

Big Emotional Experience = Big Change

Unless people go through some moving emotional experience, they won't change. A person who doesn't have money won't change. But if someone insults his family due to their poverty, that person will do whatever it takes to be successful.

Big events have that magic. Often, when team members sit in a convention and see people win, people who have less talent and less skill, or people who join later than them, it really moves them emotionally, and when they come back, they no longer accept defeat.

FOCUS ON SALES OR RECRUITS?

What's the difference between our system versus most of the industry?

The industry focuses on sales. We focus on recruits.

Which one is better? You know our preference.

SALE	RECRUIT
Spend time	Invest Time
Linear Income	Team Income
Linear Growth	Geometric Growth
Instant Income	Long Term Overrides
Slow Duplication	Faster Duplication
A Select Few	Everybody
Today's Sale	Vision for the Future
Personal Skill	Team Effort
Your Own Market	Recruits'/Team's Market
No System Needed	System is the Key
Hunter	Farmer
Wants High Contract	Wants High Override
Lonely	Member of a Team
Talks about Products	Talks about Building
Buys Leads	Does Prospect List
Mostly Full-Time	Part/Full/All-the-Time
Glass Ceiling	Unlimited Potential
Self Motivated	Team Motivated

We aim for recruits. We focus on building. As the system flows, those who go through this process may join or buy from us based on their own needs and desires. The difference is that we want to work with large numbers of people to open up more outlets.

> **IT'S SIMPLE:**
> The hunter has to look for food everyday, while the farmer takes time to breed, feed, plant, grow, and harvest.

3 WAYS TO MAKE MONEY

1. Make money through your own effort

You make money first through your own personal effort, out in the field recruiting, selling, setting the pace, and leading by example.

2. Make money through other people's efforts

When your team duplicates and follows you, you are able to make money through your team.

3. Make money make money for you

Once you begin to accumulate money, your understanding of how money works can help you have money work to build wealth for you.

THE POWER OF DUPLICATION

You can change your career in a very short period of time—as long as you do it first, and you duplicate it to your people. You must have a duplication mentality.

EACH ONE GETS ONE A WEEK

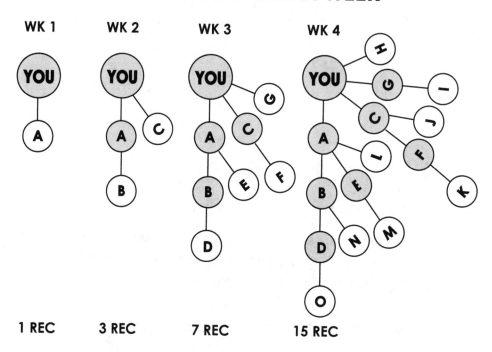

- ▶ If you recruit 1 a week and ask every new recruit to do the same, by the fourth week, you'll have 15 recruits.

- ▶ If you do the same thing with licensed agents, and each gets 1 sale a week, you'll have a lot of sales.

- ▶ If you ask everybody to go get prospect lists, you'll have an explosion.

THE MISERABLE DOCTOR

In old China, there was a great doctor. He was so good that he could cure almost any illness and all wounds. The king loved him and kept him close by. He brought the doctor with him every time he went to the battlefield, so that he could treat his generals and soldiers.

Despite his success, the doctor was unhappy and complained frequently. One day, he went up to the mountain to visit a famous monk for advice. He asked, "Master, I have a terrible job. Every time I treat a soldier or cure a general's wound, they recover. And yet shortly after, many of them get wounded again and come back to me for more treatment. The work is endless. Worst of all, some of the soldiers I treat go back to the battlefield and get killed. The more I do, the more they get hurt, the more they die! Can you help me solve this problem?"

The monk opened his eyes and said, "You're such a stupid doctor. Everyone has a job to do. The soldier's job is to fight for his kingdom. The doctor's job is to treat the wounded. The soldier does his dangerous job without complaints. Why do you complain about doing your job?"

BUILDER'S NOTE:

A frequent complaint from many people in the business is:

"Why do I have to keep recruiting when they keep quitting the business? Is there any way I can keep people from quitting?"

You can't change human nature. Like anything in life, people join and quit, whether it's a job, a business, a sports team, or a club.

You just keep recruiting. Those who stay will stay. Those who quit will quit.

YOU'RE ONE RECRUIT AWAY FROM AN EXPLOSION

"One recruit equals infinity."

You are always one recruit away from an explosion because the minute that recruit decides to get to work, the potential is unlimited. A fired up recruit will get good prospect lists and do BMPs and BPMs, which create more recruits, and from there anything is possible.

FOR EXAMPLE:

Your 1 Recruit	=	250 Names
250 Names	=	50 BMP/BPMs
50 BMP/BPMs	=	10 Recruits
Their 10 Recruits	=	2,500 Names
2,500 Names	=	500 BMP/BPMs
500 BMP/BPMs	=	100 Recruits
Their 100 Recruits	=	25,000 Names
25,000 Names	=	5,000 BMP/BPMs
5,000 BMP/BPMs	=	1,000 Recruits
Thus, 1 Recruit	=	Infinity

Events too! You're one event away from an explosion. Put popcorn to the fire. When the first one pops, the rest will explode! Bring your team to the big event. They will pop!

BUILDING

*There are a lot of great
builders in the world
who build buildings, vehicles,
hardware, and software.
We build people.
We change people's lives
as well as our life.
Building a person from
nobody to somebody
is one of the greatest miracles
in this business.
You don't have to change the world.
First, change your world,
then help someone
change their world.*

THE HEART AND MIND OF A BUILDER

Duplication	The Mind of a Builder
1. Simple	1. Recruiting Mentality
2. Clear	2. Fast Start Mentality
3. Fast	3. Meeting Mentality
4. Doable	4. Teamwork Mentality

The Builder Mindset

A great builder must develop four strong mentalities. Just like a chair with four legs, each foundation is equally important.

Builders are not born. They are built.

A builder mind does not come into existence by accident. It must be shaped and formed through years of training, experience, and focus. You must have a system to build the builder mindset.

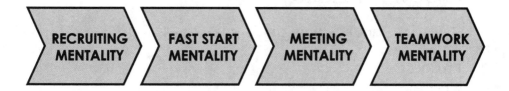

The System Flow does just that. Every step in the system is geared toward building these four mentalities.

HOW DO YOU RATE YOURSELF AND YOUR TEAM ON THESE FOUR MENTALITIES?

1. It's not the number of recruits. It's the belief and enthusiasm of the recruiter.

2. It's not the fast start. It's the habit of the trainer.

3. It's not the meeting. It's the attitude of the builder at the meeting/event.

4. It's not the teamwork. It's the trust between all the players to help the team win.

Recruiting Mentality

"We are in the recruiting business."

▶ Prospect

▶ Contact

▶ Follow up

▶ Presentation

You must have a large numbers mentality. A big prospect list, daily contact, drop by/stop by, consistent follow up, and presentations are the keys.

"Talk to many people many times."

We are in the distribution business. We are in the opening outlets business. We are in the recruiting business. Recruiting is our strength, our marketing strategy, to feed potential builders into our MD factory.

Fast Start Mentality

"A matter of life and death in building."

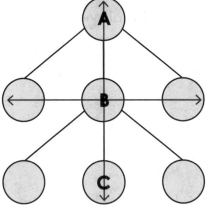

▶ Speed width

▶ Speed depth

Fast start is retention. Recruit and retain is our business building purpose. If you recruit a lot but can't retain them, it's a big waste of time. Once you fast start a new recruit—take him out to the field, recruit one person for him or show him how we help one family with our concepts and products—you lock him in. You make a believer out of him.

Fast start 3 wide to get 1 to go deep. Repeat. Duplicate it over and over.

3-3-30 is the Fast Start system to go wide to go deep. The deeper you are, the wider you will be. Can you go 20, 30, 40 deep? The deeper the root, the taller the tree.

No fast start, no width nor depth. Slow start is where all the problems are created. Slow start is a habit, so is fast start. Fast start everybody. However, you can only fast start the one who wants to fast start. Motivate and maintain the slow start people.

All you need is 3 fast start trainers to build a good baseshop. If you have 5 fast start trainers, you will have a big baseshop. If you have 10 fast start trainers, you will have a giant baseshop. Fast start is totally in the habit of the trainer.

Meeting Mentality

"The most difficult challenge."

Meeting mentality is the foundation of building. This is probably the toughest challenge of the system builder. Meetings build people's minds. It takes years to build the knowledge and the belief of a builder. Meetings and events are the classrooms for the entrepreneur. It's a leadership factory school.

Meeting mentality is monitoring mentality. Always pay attention to the number of teammates at all meetings and events. The number in attendance determines the size of your business.

BPM:

How many team members bring guests?

How many team members show up twice a week?

How many stay for the meeting after the meeting: MD Club, Manager's Meeting?

Who's predictable? Who's always there?

Who's unpredictable?

LOCAL EVENT:

How many team members attend?

Who fights for recognition?

Who are the rising stars?

Who mobilizes the team to come early?

Who volunteers for the event?

BIG EVENT:

Which team is well organized and well prepared?

Which team has the most number of team members/spouses who attend?

How disciplined is the team? Who endures? Who falls? Who is distracted?

Who makes a commitment to change, to build, to go full time?

Teamwork Mentality

"Before you build a team, you must be a team player first."

The foundation of team building:

▶ A high level of trust

▶ A common goal

▶ Sacrifice/volunteering

"Are you a system builder or a system user?

Are you a giver or a taker?"

As a team player, you develop the critical teamwork mentality. When you give yourself to the success of the team, you understand the dynamic of winning.

You must be trustworthy. You should never make a decision based on your personal interest alone. Anything you do, you do for the team, for the success of the whole organization.

You must have team building efforts:

▶ Home meetings and gatherings

▶ Team competition

Teamwork happens when you have:

▶ A clear vision

▶ A strong mission

▶ The will to win

A non-team player will hardly believe that he can build a big team. Best team players are best team builders.

GIANT STEP

3-3-30   FAST START TO MD CLUB

5-5-30   SYSTEM TRAINER

10-10-30   GLG/MD BASESHOP BUILDER

30-30-100   WORLD SYSTEM BUILDER

"Duplicate your way to success!"

FOUNDATION OF BUILDING
BUILD IT RIGHT, BUILD IT STRONG

Recruiting is the foundation of building. The sale comes next. Then you motivate your team. Last, you build them to become the leaders of the future.

However, Many People Did Not Build It Right

▶ Some people recruit a lot yet have few sales.

▶ Some focus too much on sales and lack recruits.

▶ Some try so hard to motivate people but forgot to recruit and sell.

▶ Some keep teaching, training, and building a handful of old people, yet the whole base lacks recruits, sales, and motivation.

What Does Your Baseshop Look Like?

A builder's team must always focus on strong recruits and strong sales. Only then will motivation and building become possible.

As a leader, you must always maintain a strong foundation and a healthy balance. If the team lacks recruits, you must personally recruit, do PPLs, BMPs, and BPMs to crank up recruiting momentum.

If the team has recruits but ends up with fewer sales, you must work with your trainers to go out in the field, match them up, manage their activities, and follow up on their results.

If you consistently have recruits and sales but produce no leaders and no MDs, you must work on identifying potential MDs and overlapping leadership to build new potential stars.

FAST START AND DUPLICATION

Everything you do, whether it's a recruiting presentation, a sale, or the second interview, these are the four essential ingredients you need to duplicate people.

INGREDIENTS FOR DUPLICATION

1. Simple
2. Clear
3. Fast
4. Easy

▶ Take field training, for example. When a new trainee goes out in the field with you, they must see you keeping everything simple. There is no duplication in complication. Remember: A new trainee is just like a student on their first day in class.

▶ You must also be consistent in order to make it clear. If you are not consistent, if you are constantly changing your presentation or procedure, confusion will set in. There will be no duplication.

▶ You must do it fast. The nature of duplication is speed. You can't make a copy of something that goes slow. Nobody will be duplicated if you move like a snail.

▶ Lastly, it must be easy. If they see that it's easy to duplicate, they will stay. But if it looks difficult, they don't think they can do it, so they quit.

Among the four ingredients—simple, clear, fast and easy— guess which is the most important factor?

Fast. Speed is the most critical factor. The reason is that if we do it slow, most new recruits will quit the business sooner than you think. At that point, it doesn't matter how simple, clear, and easy you make it. The new recruit won't be around to see it anyway.

"Speed duplication is the key."

You must fast start a new recruit in the first 24 to 48 hours. If you wait for a week, by that time they will have had enough of rejection and disappointment. They either quit or are reluctant to go out in the field.

BUILDING FUNDAMENTALS

"You must build at least 5 to 7 strong direct builders."

You don't want to recruit 5 to 7 people in your team. You don't want to have 5 to 7 salespeople working for you. What you want is to build 5 to 7 builder legs.

You must go through a lot of prospects and recruits and work with them to find these builders.

The only way for you to build wide is to commit to do it personally. Nobody will do it for you. You can't wait for your upline to do it. And you can't wait for your downline to do it.

If you wait for your upline to do it for you, prepare to get in line. They have to work on their business too.

If you wait for your downline to do it, prepare to get disappointed. They're waiting for you.

By the way, in any business, nobody expects the higher-ups or the subordinates to do things for them.

How To Go Wide?

You do these relentlessly:

- Prospect
- Contact
- Drop By / Stop By
- Invite
- Pick prospect up
- Do BMP
- Do BPM

▶ Make appointments

▶ Do business interview

▶ Fast start them to MD Club

▶ PPL them at home

▶ Do financial strategy (or, if you are not licensed, ask someone licensed to do it)

▶ Follow up, drop by, call them, remind them, and remind them again

▶ Then find another person and repeat the same process all over again

Sound like a lot of work? Yes, it is.

You must BMP and BPM consistently. Always have guests, and always do presentations. You keep doing it until you find your first superstar, your first MD, your first builder. Once you get your first, the second will be easier.

But:

"What if I'm still new? I don't know how to do the BMP?" Just do it, and you will learn.

"What if I'm scared? I'm afraid to take someone to the BPM." Just do it, and you won't be scared anymore.

"How do I make an appointment?" Just ask.

"Doing the interview? I've never done a recruiting interview in my life!" Just do it. You're the "boss" now. It's your business.

BUILD DEEP

"Every 4 deep, you may get one builder."

Like a tree or a building, unless it goes deep, it won't stand.

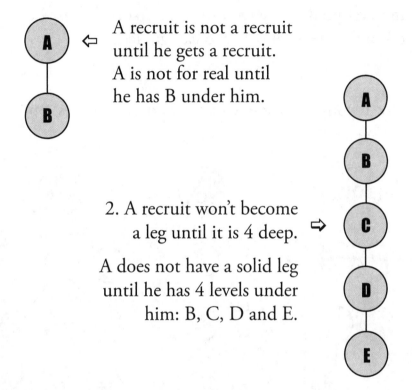

A recruit is not a recruit until he gets a recruit. A is not for real until he has B under him.

2. A recruit won't become a leg until it is 4 deep.

A does not have a solid leg until he has 4 levels under him: B, C, D and E.

Why 4 Deep? Retention Is The Main Reason

If you recruit A and A recruits nobody, if A quits, which happens often, you end up with nothing. But if A recruits B, A probably won't quit because he's excited about having a team member. And even if A does quit, you still have B left. Same goes for the leg. If you go 4 deep, most likely, all A, B, C, and D will stay because they have people under them. And even if one or two of them quit, you will still have enough people left to build with.

WIDE AND DEEP

"You go wide to go deep."

Go Wide To Go Deep

You can never go deep by recruiting 1 person. Often you must recruit 3 to 4 wide to find 1 who can go deep.

4 x 4

Normally, if you go 4 wide, you can find 1 who goes 4 deep.

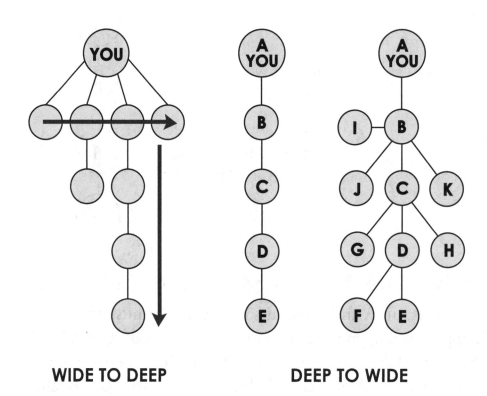

WIDE TO DEEP   DEEP TO WIDE

Go Deep To Go Wide

Assuming you have 4 deep first, you will be wide anyway.

To illustrate (see graphic on previous page): If D has E, D's excited and will get one more person, F.

If C has D, E and F under him, he will be fired up to get G and H.

If B has C, D, E, F, G and H, he will be super hot and go wide with I, J, and K.

That's why you should always go wide to go deep and always go deep to go wide. In other words, recruit personally and help your team recruit.

"Since you build anyway, why not build it big?"

Focus On Building Deep

SCENARIO I

SCENARIO II

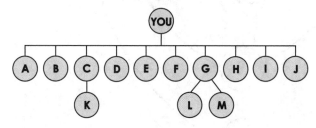

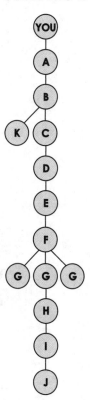

In scenario I, although you have 10 wide, you only have 2 people, C and G, going deep, so the organization is not stable.

In scenario II, everyone in the organization, from A to I, is quite solid because they have someone under them.

Going deep requires the upline to taproot down. This creates a builder's mindset, a recruit-to-build mentality.

Duplication

A never duplicates himself until B can take care of C, C can take care of D, and so on.

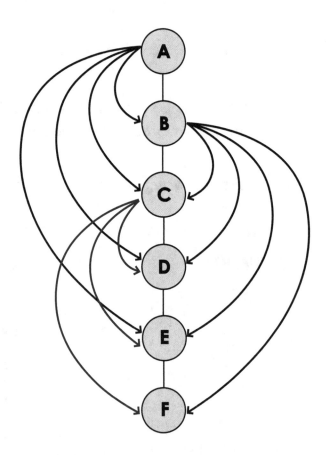

Build wide for profitability.

Build deep for long term security.

MD CLUB
FOR WIDE AND DEEP

MD Club is a system to build wide and deep. Every new recruit in our system wants to recruit 3 to become MD Club as soon as possible. Thus, he has a recruit wide mentality from the get go.

At the same time, every one of these new 3 members knows that they too will recruit 3 to qualify for MD Club. As a result, the MD Club system will build deep immediately.

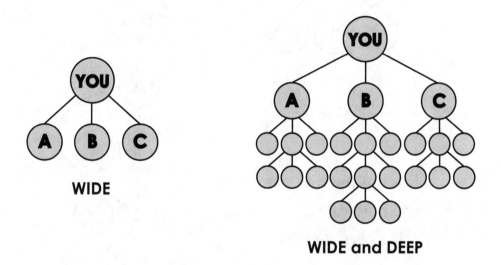

WIDE

WIDE and DEEP

This is powerful because the system is designed to create both width and depth.

DUPLICATE
THE DUPLICATOR

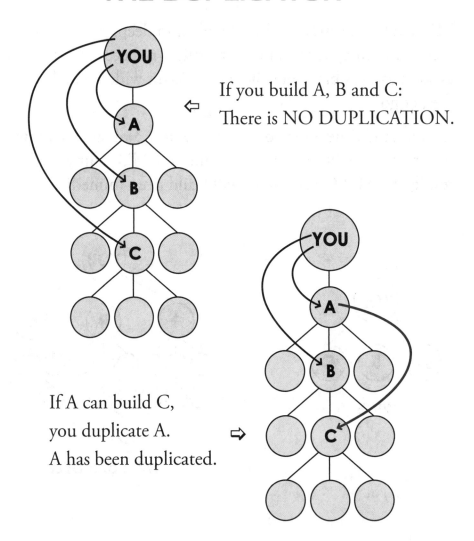

If you build A, B and C:
There is NO DUPLICATION.

If A can build C,
you duplicate A.
A has been duplicated.

The MD Club system also builds builders. You build MD Club and once the MD Club can build another MD Club, she learns to become a good builder and a good duplicator.

Remember: Every MD Club member not only recruits 3 people but should also observe 3 complete sales presentations (3-3-30).

BUILDING AND GROWING

"Everybody in the base, wide or deep, is your direct."

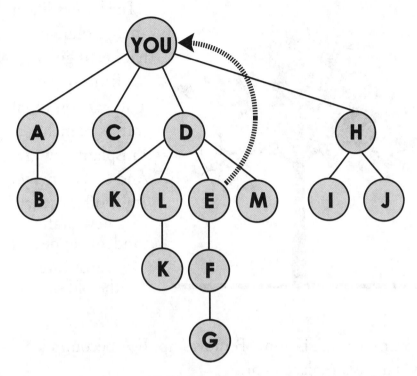

Let's look at D's leg. E is direct to D. But if D quits the business, E will be your direct. On the other hand, if D becomes big and qualifies for MD, and E is the replacement leg, E will eventually be your direct anyway.

So treat everybody in the base as your direct. Don't think that G is too deep under you because he's under F, E, and D. Treat G, F, E like your direct. You work with them, PPL, field train, motivate, build them, and treat everybody the same.

This Is The Dynamic Of The Base

Picture this:
The base is like a magic orange tree that keeps giving you fruit forever.
It allows you to take off its branches to transplant new trees.
And every time you take off a branch, a new branch suddenly appears to substitute the old one.

For example: If A is gone, B moves up. If A becomes a MD, B moves up as a replacement.

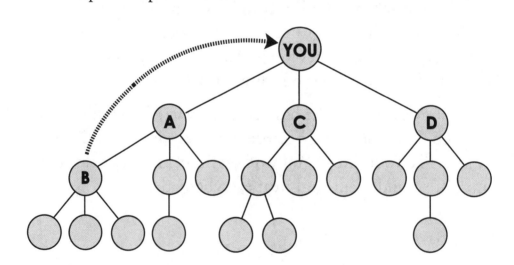

Replacement

The replacement leg, or exchange leg, makes our system unique. It's the ultimate secret of our success.

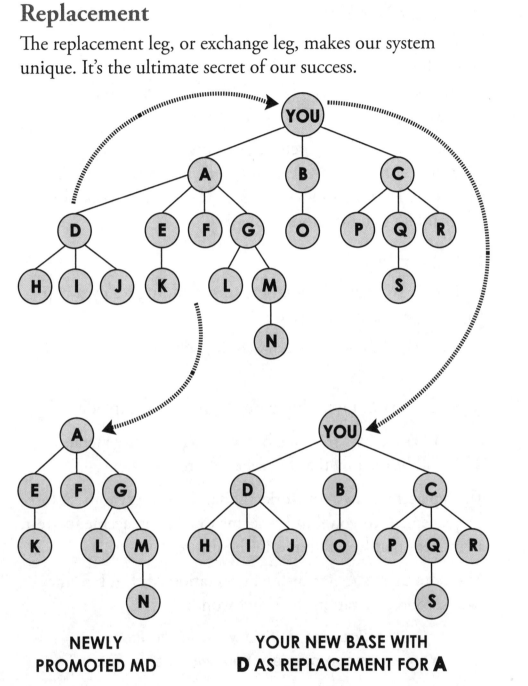

NEWLY PROMOTED MD

YOUR NEW BASE WITH D AS REPLACEMENT FOR A

As you can see, when A becomes a MD, you get D's leg as a replacement.

Is It Fair For You?

It's fair for you because you recruited A. A knew nothing about the business when he joined. Then you helped A recruit D, E, F, G, H, I, J, K, L, M, and N. It's A's team, but it's also your team too.

You built him up. You spent time, money, and a lot of effort for A and all his 4 legs. When he leaves your baseshop to become MD, he still has 3 legs, E, F, G. So it's good for him, and it's good for you.

Is It Fair For A?

It's fair for A because A will now start building his own base and take replacement legs too.

Let's look at A's new team a few months later on. (See graphic on next page.)

Assume F and G do nothing, but E grows and explodes.

Now A has a new MD. He's happy to have a 1st generation MD, and he's happy that he has K as a replacement.

The replacement system works the same for everybody. A lost a replacement to you, but he begins to take replacements from all the legs that he will build in the future.

Also note that as A gets his first generation MD, E becomes your second generation. Isn't that wonderful?

> *"Replacement, it's a win-win situation.*
> *You exchange one leg. You will receive many."*

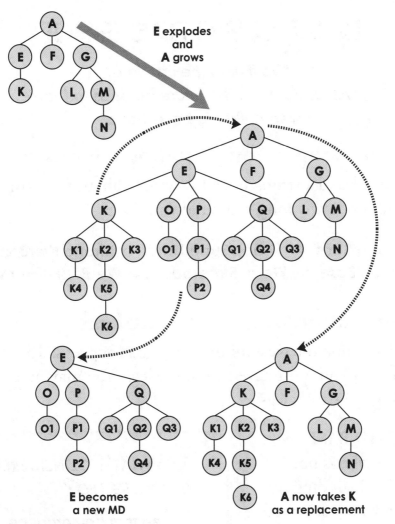

E explodes
and
A grows

E becomes
a new MD

A now takes K
as a replacement

Strong Replacement

When you become a MD, you should give your upline your strongest leg, so that you will feel good taking the strongest leg of your future MDs later on.

When you promote a MD, you should take a strong leg for replacement, so that your baseshop continues to be strong.

However, if you give and take weak replacement legs, be prepared to deal with a weak, crippled organization.

"I'd rather give up 1 strong leg to get 10 strong legs in the future than give up 1 weak leg to get 10 weak ones."

BUILD A BIG BASESHOP

"Do it right the first time.
It will last forever. The future belongs to those
who build big baseshops."

The Baseshop Is Your Building Foundation

You must build a strong base. Everything about this business depends on how strong you build your base.

> Strong Base ⇨ Strong Superbase ⇨ Strong Hierarchy
> Weak Base ⇨ Weak Superbase ⇨ Weak Hierarchy

Build A Mininum Of 3 Strong Legs

Your base should have a minimum of 3 strong legs. This means that you must have a lot more legs. You may need 10 legs to get 3 strong legs.

NON-MD BASE: Anyone who is not a MD yet, including the person who just joined. This is very important. If you build a strong non-MD base, you will build a strong MD base. But if you don't do it right, forget about becoming a MD.

> ## What's considered a strong leg?
>
> *The leg that can produce double-digit recruits and double-digit sales in a month every month.*

ACT LIKE A MD NOW: Too many people keep playing the "I-don't-know, I'm-not-good-enough, I'm-not-ready-yet" game when they start building the business. Everybody has to start somewhere. So did your MD. So why don't you start doing things like her? Do everything the MD does. Only when you are really stuck should you ask her for help.

Prospect, recruit, hire, sell, do paperwork, order supplies, book for conventions, motivate the team, go out of your way to do things, and don't expect your upline to do things for your baseshop. You take care of your own base.

MD Base Standards

In my opinion, good recruiting numbers are:

▶ Average: 25 recruits / month

▶ Good: 50 recruits / month

▶ Great: 100 recruits / month

In my opinion, good production is:

▶ Average: 25 sales / 50K production / month

▶ Good: 50 sales / 100K production / month

▶ Great: 100 sales / 200K production / month

Things You Need To Do In The Base

MAKE MONEY: You must make money. Not only for your family, but the base requires you to set a good example of success for the team. You should hit a minimum six-figure annual income.

GO OUT IN THE FIELD: It's not an option. You must go out in the field everyday if you want to build the base. The baseshop will collapse if the MD doesn't go out field training.

THE ENVIRONMENT: The baseshop environment is critical. MoZone must be in motion. There should be no negativity and no distractions.

THE BUSINESS MACHINE: The purpose of building a base is to build a business machine. Every day, every night, every meeting, sell the business. You sell products to clients, but you sell the business to the team.

> *You can do anything–BPM, paperwork, training, motivation–but if you don't do field training prospecting, field training recruiting, and field training sales, the base will be crippled.*

THE CRUSADE FACTORY: The other purpose of building a base is to create crusaders. We get together as a base to join hands and go out to fulfill our mission as a team. Always do it right, and do it with pride. Do good things for people.

TREAT EVERYBODY WELL: Treat your team members and your clients with care and respect. Both have to go together.

MAINTAIN THE SPIRIT OF THE TEAM:

> *If you share an office with other bases, they must also be positive and must not distract your team.*

If you fail to create teamwork in the base, you will have big trouble later on with the hierarchy. In the people business, everybody is different and tends to do things on their own. Your main job is to build a team. That is when all things become possible.

"Build a team. Sell the dream."

BIG BASESHOP MENTALITY

Big baseshop is a mentality, so is small baseshop.

▶ You must have an unwavering determination to build a big base. You cannot give up. You must persist and build it up until you get what you want.

▶ You must set a clear goal for the size of a big base. For example, 50 recruits and 100K production per month or 100 recruits and 200K production per month.

▶ Focus on the trainer. It's not the size of the base. It's the "size" of the trainers in the base.

An average trainer can do 5 recruits and 5 sales per month.

Thus, if you have:

10 trainers =
50 rec / 50 sales

20 trainers =
100 rec / 100 sales

30 trainers = 150 rec / 150 sales

> *A trainer is someone who can do the presentation, recruit, sell, and most importantly duplicate the new trainee in a systematized way.*

Big baseshops have great alignment of trainers and leaders who agree that their mission is to be part of a big base. They know that when they grow up in a big base, they will also build their own big baseshops in the future.

"The ultimate purpose of a big base is to create a factory to build future big baseshop builders."

A COMMITMENT TO BUILD

*"You must wake up everyday
thinking about how to grow your business."*

Your ultimate goal is to build a lot of builders. They are the leaders who run a strong baseshop, a strong superbase, and a strong superteam.

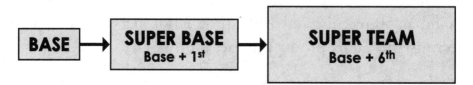

These are your businesses, your outlets, your cash flow machine. First year, become MD. Second year, build a strong base. Third year, build superbase. The fourth year and beyond, grow a big hierarchy.

You may recruit a lot, sell a lot, and make good money for now. But if in the future you have no MDs and no builders, you will have wasted your valuable time because you failed to build anything long lasting.

Without builders and without MDs, you will still have to go to work everyday to make a living. Your overrides will diminish to little or nothing. And your team will shrink and eventually disappear.

> **Three to five years from now, what's your business going to look like? How many MDs and builders will you have in your organization?**

RECRUIT TO BUILD

*You must know the
reason why you recruit.*
▶ **Do you recruit to recruit?**
▶ **Do you recruit to sell?**
▶ **Do you recruit to build?**

1. Recruit To Recruit

The emphasis of recruit, recruit, recruit sometimes creates an attitude of recruiting blindly for the purpose of having the maximum number of people join. A lot of people recruit when we have contests or when they want to qualify for an event. The problem is that they do this for the sole purpose of recruiting, and not much happens after that. Other people want to recruit a lot hoping that a superstar will fall from the sky.

2. Recruit To Sell

When you recruit, the sales will follow. But if that's the only reason you recruit, this kind of thinking is more or less a salesperson mentality.

3. Recruit To Build

The true purpose of recruiting is neither to recruit nor to sell but rather to build outlets, to build MDs, to build builders. Therefore, you recruit to build and run the system. Then more recruits and more sales will result from your building efforts.

LADDER OF FOCUS

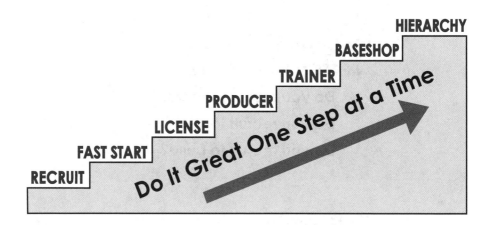

STEP 1 - RECRUIT: A new recruit is a great starting point, but it won't be of any good unless the new recruit follows this ladder of focus with urgency.

STEP 2 - FAST START: A new recruit must accomplish steps 1, 2, and 3—PPL, BMP + BPM, PFS—within the first 30 days of joining and complete 3-3-30 to qualify for MD Club.

This fast start is so critical for the new person.

> *"A recruit is not for real until she finishes the fast start and qualifies for MD Club."*

STEP 3 - LICENSE: A new recruit should start the licensing process as soon as possible. Many people delay the licensing process and drag it on too long. Without a license, she can't talk about products, make sales, or make money. Most people who are slow in this step rarely survive the business. Lack of focus and lack of desire are the main problems.

On the other hand, there is a reverse problem when someone comes in, just focuses on licensing, doesn't want to go through steps 1, 2, 3, doesn't qualify for MD Club, and has no team. These people skip the system and rarely make it because what can someone do when they have a license but no recruits, no prospects, and no understanding of the system?

STEP 4 - PRODUCER: A good producer makes 4 to 10 sales a month and makes good money on a part-time basis.

STEP 5 - TRAINER: If the trainee is a good producer, chances are she can be a good trainer too. However, if she is a good producer but not a good trainer, she cannot duplicate herself. Good trainers will train the trainers that will build the foundation of a big baseshop.

A good trainer is not just good in making sales. A good trainer is someone who can take a new trainee out to help them do BMP/BPM, present the financial concepts and the PFS, and close the sale. In short, a good trainer can duplicate herself.

STEP 6 - BASESHOP BUILDER: The baseshop is where everything happens. This is where she starts building a recruiting, building, and motivation factory that trains, shapes, and molds future producers, future trainers, and future baseshop builders.

STEP 7 - HIERARCHY BUILDER: As she maintains and builds a big baseshop, she will promote new MDs coming out of her base. She needs to build a strong front line. Strong first generation MDs will help her build a big hierarchy.

1. A recruit is not a recruit until she fast starts MD Club 3-3-30.

2. A MD Club without a license will be useless and lose momentum. A licensed person without fast start has no foundation and will usually have no place to go.

3. A licensed person must become a good personal producer and make money.

4. A good producer sharpens her skills to become a good trainer.

5. A good trainer will be able to train new people and duplicate herself.

6. Good trainers build big baseshops.

7. Big baseshop builders build big hierarchies.

DON'T BE A REGULAR BUILDER, BE A SYSTEM BUILDER

Regular Builder	System Builder
◆ Works in the business	■ Works on business
◆ Depends on the system	■ Builds the system
◆ Lives in a built house	■ Builds a house to live in
◆ Waits for BPM	■ Everyday is a BPM day
◆ Waits for upline	■ Waits for nobody
◆ Builds step-by-step	■ Stumbles forward
◆ Small picture/small dream	■ Big picture/big dream
◆ Tries-to-learn attitude	■ Start-up-a-company attitude
◆ Takes 3 years to understand the business	■ Takes 3 months to understand the business
◆ Weak, reserved, negative most the time	■ Strong, excited, positive all the time
◆ Slow decision-maker	■ Quick decision-maker
◆ Uncoachable	■ Coachable
◆ Doesn't see themself opening an office	■ Dying to open their own office

BUILDABLE PRODUCT

"Keep it simple. Keep it duplicatable."

Imagine if McDonald's sold gourmet food like steak and lobster. They would have to change their kitchens all over the world. They would have to retrain all their workers on how to cook a steak rare, medium rare, medium well, and well done. The complexity could cause the whole system to collapse.

Steak and seafood are not buildable products for McDonald's. But hamburgers and fries are. I'm not an expert in the kitchen, but I'm guessing their kitchens can't cook many different kinds of dishes. In any case, they probably don't want to. They want to keep things simple. The simplicity of their system allows them to duplicate and multiply.

McDonald's keeps it simple. They sell hamburgers, fries, and soft drinks. Starbucks too. Coffee is their thing. Jamba Juice just does juice. KFC focuses on chicken.

The hamburger is the buildable product of McDonald's. Coffee is the buildable product of Starbucks. Chicken is the buildable product of KFC. Juice is the buildable product of Jamba Juice.

McDonald's doesn't mind if their customers go to Jamba Juice for better drinks. They also don't mind if customers think their chicken nuggets can't compete with KFC's wings and drumsticks.

"Focus on your core business.
There is enough business for everybody."

It is unbelievable to see that there are people in the building and duplication business who can't keep it simple.

It is amazing how complicated some people are becoming, as if they're trying to do everything for everybody. They learn everything, compare everything, but recruit nobody and sell nothing.

> **System builders know what products their business can build on, what's buildable and what's non-buildable.**

Even if they recruit someone, their recruit will be dead on arrival. They scare the new recruit with all the products they hype up. These people always get excited about something new. Everybody's always excited. They go out and get all kinds of licenses, gather all kinds of materials—brochures, prospectuses, software—and get together with other teammates to study the new products and services. They bring in all kinds of vendors and wholesalers to their office. This week Mr. A of company A says their product is the best, so the team gets excited. Next week, Mr. B of company B shows them their product is actually better, so the team gets more excited. The week after that, they bring in Mr. C, who claims that their product has even more benefits. Then next week, they talk about health insurance, then Property & Casualty, then mortgages.

They go out to see clients and unload all the things they learned, all the products they offer. Then when they can't make money, they bring in the self-help guru, attend motivational seminars, and buy books on how to be a winner, a leader, a super salesperson, and a visionary. When all these things don't work, they visit the fortune teller or the feng shui master to learn how to rearrange office furniture, so they can change their destiny.

Can You Focus On One Thing At A Time?

Can you make one thing work first before jumping into another deal? If you try to master everything, you master nothing. Worse, your team can't duplicate you. And if they don't think they can do it, they won't stay. The "jack of all trades" won't become big and can't duplicate anybody.

Also, if you flip flop from one thing to the next, your team won't know what you truly believe in. You must be consistent with your message and your actions.

For example, some people get very excited when the market is up but become so depressed when the market goes down. Do you still remember when you preached the virtues of dollar cost averaging and diversification? If you truly believe in our mission, you must be consistent. You can't sell something one day when it's hot and go sell other things when it's not so hot.

*"Focus on your mission and persist
in your actions."*

On your journey through life, if you keep loading your wagon with things you pick up along the way, someday your vehicle will become heavier and slower. With all this baggage, how are you going to get through hills and mountains? How can you move fast? Are you willing to unload these things?

BUILDING LONG DISTANCE

Why should you build long distance? There are millions of people around you. You can work your lifetime in your local area and never run out of recruits or sales. But there will be times when you need to go the distance.

1. It's The People, Not The Location

Sometimes you can't find the right people in your local area because the superstars are out of town. In fact, you never know where your biggest builders live. This happened to me and many other builders too.

> *"It's not the size of the city.*
> *It's the size of the leader that counts."*

2. You Have Time And Your Team Is Not That Busy

Most of the time, you're not always that busy. You can squeeze an extra 1 or 2 days out of the week. In addition, most of your team has free time. Why not be more efficient?

3. You And Your Team Must Get Out Of Your Comfort Zones

Building long distance forces you to work harder. It forces you to do more BPMs, training, and business interviews. It's tough, but you grow faster.

4. Greater Vision

Building long distance stretches your vision. You think bigger.

5. Better Strategy

When you build long distance, you are more strategic in your actions, planning and preparing before acting, because you don't want to waste precious time.

6. You Get The Ping Pong Effect

Building long distance will lead to more referrals and cross-recruiting from different locations. It will multiply your growth.

For example: Assume there is a new airline carrier.

1. The airline starts to fly between two cities: San Jose and Los Angeles.

SJ ⇨ LA

LA ⇨ SJ

SJ ⟷ LA

2 cities = 2 ways

2. The airline adds Houston to their schedule.

SJ ⇨ LA   LA ⇨ SJ

SJ ⇨ HS   HS ⇨ SJ

LA ⇨ HS   HS ⇨ LA

3 cities = 6 ways

3. The airline adds New York.

SJ ⇨ LA   SJ ⇨ NY   HS ⇨ LA

LA ⇨ SJ   NY ⇨ SJ   LA ⇨ HS

SJ ⇨ HS   LA ⇨ NY   NY ⇨ HS

HS ⇨ SJ   NY ⇨ LA   HS ⇨ NY

4 cities = 12 ways

It's easier to have exponential growth by building long distance because the ping pong effect creates multiplication.

THE NATURE OF A LONG DISTANCE TEAM

"There are great advantages to working with people at a distance."

1. THEY APPRECIATE YOU MORE. You make an effort to see your long-distance team, while your local people see you everyday and take you for granted.

2. THEY'RE MORE EAGER TO LEARN. They're hungry for information and training. They never seem to get enough.

3. THEY'RE MORE COACHABLE. Of course, they have to be, or else you may not come back.

4. THEY'RE MORE INDEPENDENT. They have no choice. They have no one to depend on. So they do more work by themselves.

5. THEY DON'T COMPLAIN. If they do, you're not around to hear it anyway.

6. THEY ACCEPT REALITY. They experience the difficulty of the business sooner than if you held them by the hand from the day they joined.

7. THEY ALWAYS ASK YOU TO VISIT. They need you more than you need them.

8. THEY'RE WILLING TO PERFORM. They entice you with results for you to come back.

9. THEY'RE WILLING TO TRAVEL LIKE YOU. In the future, they tend to build long distance like you.

10. YOUR LOCAL TEAM BEGINS TO APPRECIATE YOU MORE AND NEEDS YOU MORE. As they say, "You don't know what you got till it's gone."

11. YOUR LOCAL TEAM BECOMES MORE INDEPENDENT. They realize they can't rely on you all the time.

12. YOU CREATE MORE COMPETITION. More good news comes from different locations.

REFERRAL PROGRAM

If you're not ready to build long distance, or the new recruit at a distance is not ready, don't do it.

Instead you should refer your prospect to a local MD to take care of them and work out a solution for the benefit of all parties involved.

THE CHALLENGES OF BUILDING LONG DISTANCE

1. Are You Building The Right People?

You must find out if they're the right people, if they want it bad enough.

Put them on the scale. Who wants it more? If they want you more than you want them, you win. If you want them more than they want you, you lose. If they want to win more than you want them to win, you win. If you want them to win more than they want to win, you lose.

2. Is Your Local Team Losing?

If your local team is not strong enough, they may fall apart. Travel only if you know that it won't affect the local base much. Thus, don't leave your base too long. In the early days, travel only 1 or 2 days a week and increase your time away later on when you see fit.

3. Cost

Building long distance is a big investment of time and money. Make sure you can afford it. Make sure you're serious. Make sure the long distance team is serious. They must make your time well worth it by scheduling a lot of field training, so they can learn faster and duplicate new trainers.

HOW FAR DO YOU WANT TO GO?

"This is a long run, not a sprint."

When building long distance, try to limit your travel to no more than 3 days at a time. From my experience, we can compress a week's worth of work into 3 days. If you have to spend more than 3 days at a certain place, that location, team, or leader is probably not good enough to meet with you halfway. They may not want it bad enough, or they are just too weak and dependent to survive in the business.

They must also schedule enough appointments for you to do field training. You can't just go away and come home empty-handed. They can't expect you to spend money and time away from your family for them, and yet they do not do their part to make your effort pay off.

Develop a habit of taking care of your family first and the business second. If you have to choose between a business event and a family event, pick the family event.

Does it mean that we won't make sacrifices sometimes? Of course, we do. There were times that I missed family events, but most of them were not important. I judged between the two: If the family event was not that important, I would pick the business event. After all, I'm doing it for my family.

BUILDING PEOPLE

Imagine building a house and having all the building blocks and beams, but forgetting the cement, the glue, and the nails that bind them together.

"Build with your heart.
The cement puts all the building blocks together."

You may have early success. You may have large numbers of recruits, lots of sales, and impressive titles. You may dazzle people with your big house, your fancy car, and your expensive toys. But if you don't understand how to build people, you won't make it in the business over the long haul.

Build Yourself First

Before you can build people, you must build yourself first. It's a two-way street between you and your teammate. What do you bring to the table? If you are strong, they will be strong. If you are weak and uncommitted, don't expect much.

Build Relationships

Know your people. Know their family. Know what they want, what's important to them.

Organize time to get together, so you can meet their spouse and their children. You may find out more about your teammates by talking to their spouse. If your spouse is involved, he or she can help you build rapport with your teammates' spouses.

They must feel that they're important to you. They're not just a code number.

"People quit a business,
but they won't quit a friend."

Build Trust

Can your people trust you? Do you say what you mean and mean what you say?

What's your reputation? Can you improve it? Are you often late to meetings? Do you forget about appointments? Do you recognize your problems or do you just ignore them?

> **YOUR PEOPLE ALWAYS WANT TO KNOW:**
> ▶ your trustworthiness
> ▶ your commitment
> ▶ your capability
> ▶ how much you care about them

When you promise people something, would you deliver if challenges arise or if you have to take a loss? In a conflicting situation between you and your people, who wins?

If it's 50/50: They win.

If it's 60/40: They win.

If it's 70/30: They win.

If it's 80/20: They win.

If it's 90/10: You win.

Only in a case where the evidence shows that you are 90% right and they are only 10% right, then the ruling should be in your favor.

For example: If you and your downline both know a guy, and you both approach him, but you are not sure who talked to him first, then the recruit should belong to your downline.

Or if you talk to the guy first, but he wants to think about it, and 10 days later on, your downline invites him to your BPM, and he joins, then he should join your downline.

Or if you invite the guy to a BPM, when he comes in and meets his best friend, who happens to be your downline, and he wants to join your downline instead of you, then your downline wins.

However, if you fly to New York to recruit the guy, and when he joins you, your downline tells you that your new recruit is his best friend, then in this case, you can tell him to back off.

"You can't win on your people.
If you win on your people, you may end up losing.
If you lose on your people, you may end up winning.
When your people win, you will win."

Be A Servant Leader

Put your people first. Put yourself last. Take care of them. Always do it first. Do it many times before you ask them to do it.

Stand up and stand by your people, especially through tough times. People may come and go. They may not appreciate you. But you always wait for them. They leave you. But you never leave them.

Always be proud of your people and be proud of your team. Everybody will be somebody, and everyone will win.

"Your commitment to the business
and your people are the key.
People won't commit until you commit."

Look For The Good Things

Everyone is different. Everyone has their own strengths and weaknesses. Everyone has good qualities and bad qualities.

Focus on their strengths and their goodness. Be like a teacher, aware of their students' weaknesses but always focused on their strengths. Praise your people and help them win.

Believe In Your People

People have tough times in the business. Your belief in them is very critical.

Do you believe in the power of believing? When was the last time somebody really believed in you? Sometimes even your family doesn't believe in you. How great does it feel when someone sincerely believes in people like you and me?

Be the one who believes in your people. I do believe the greatest gift you can give to your people is to give them your total belief that they will be successful.

Make Them Feel Good

Make people feel good about themselves. Everyone is important to you and to the team, whether they're the big shot or the new person.

Give praise and recognition for everything they do, even on small achievements. Remember when you were small?

Lift them up. Share their successes with everybody. When they feel good, they do good.

Be for real when you deal with people. Don't be "plastic fantastic", saying things you don't really mean. Of course, we need to be upbeat and excited, but let's not be phoney. Otherwise, all the building effort has no substance.

Build Confidence

Most importantly, you've got to build confidence. If you are confident about your capability, your business know-how, your team will also gain more confidence, knowing that they follow someone who knows what he is doing.

You must master the business. Of course, there will always be things that you don't know. Be sincere. Don't "wing it". If your team asks something that you are not sure about, tell them you will find out and will get back to them.

You must be committed to your goal and declare it publicly. The team needs to know what you want to achieve. Imagine a passenger gets on a ship and the captain doesn't know how to operate it and doesn't know for sure where the destination is.

> *You build yourself to build people. The more people you build, the more you build yourself.*

IN THE PEOPLE BUSINESS:

▶ You do everything but expect nothing.

▶ You do it first. They do it later.

▶ You come first. They come last.
   They leave first. You leave last.

▶ You should never win over your people.

▶ If you say ten good things and one bad thing,
   they remember only the bad thing.

▶ They can criticize you. You can't
   criticize them.

▶ They come and go, but you always stay.

▶ They do and they don't, but you
   always do it.

▶ They may win or they may lose,
   but you have to win.

▶ You need them, but you don't need them.
   You care for them, but you don't care
   for them.

HAVE A HIGH LEVEL OF TOLERANCE

"People are like the weather. They change often."

In a highly competitive world, when we want to win so badly, it's easy for us to lose patience. We lose patience with ourselves, and we lose patience with our people.

Always Give The Benefit Of The Doubt

Whenever people don't join or buy from you, or say something negative, be patient. They might have had a bad experience before. They might have personal problems. Maybe they've just undergone a crisis. Or maybe you talked to them at the wrong time on the wrong day. Don't get mad. Don't get even. Be tolerant.

When you go to the meeting and the speaker or the upline says something unpleasant, you may think they're pointing the finger at you. Give them the benefit of the doubt. Most of the time, they're probably talking about somebody else, and even if it is you, they're probably just trying to help. It could be that the way they express things is not well delivered.

When your people don't show up, when they fail to do something, when they drive you nuts, be patient. They don't intend to disappoint you.

When the paperwork is screwed up, when the commissions are incorrect, when applications are returned, be patient. It could be their mistake, or it could be your mistake. Things will work themselves out.

When things have to change, be patient. There are probably good reasons. Always give people the benefit of the doubt. Always accept people's mistakes.

"To err is human, to forgive divine."
-ALEXANDER POPE

Don't Take It Personal

When bad things can happen, they will happen. Murphy's law rules. Most of the time, problems aren't aimed at you. Don't take it personal. Don't hold grudges.

You're A Leader

You must have big shoulders. You must have the ability to absorb adversity. You must show that you're bigger than the small things. You can forgive and forget. You focus on the big task.

People Change

Most people change. They'll be better to you. They'll appreciate you. They'll understand you. If you don't hold grudges and if you don't close the door on them, they'll join you, buy from you, and follow you.

Learn To Live With People

Don't ask for separation. When disputes occur, work it out. When arguments arise, listen to one another. If both persons are right, then who is wrong? If you don't have perfect downlines, live with them. If you don't have the best uplines, live with them.

When you win, you won't remember these things anyway. When you get to the top of the mountain, you won't worry about all the tough stuff. Your people need to grow. You must have a high level of tolerance to accept their mistakes.

"Give your downline a chance.
Give your upline a chance. Give everyone a chance."

BUILDING GIANTS

*"You must build giants for long term
profitability and security."*

MD is the starting position. Some of them will develop to
become giants, World System Builders (WSB), and above.

▶ A giant is a system builder with a strong organization.

▶ A giant has ambitious vision and passion for the mission.
They stand out by their conviction and project a successful
image of their future.

▶ A giant maintains a strong baseshop and builds strong
frontline leaders. Thus he has a big super base through 1st.

▶ A giant overlaps leadership and builds a great
superteam through 6 generations. A giant is
generation blind and hierarchy blind, a pure builder.

▶ A giant has a great recruiting mentality and a
builder's mindset and maintains a strong recruiting
and building machine throughout his organization.

▶ A giant masters the meeting and events.

▶ A giant is consistent and predictable.

▶ A giant is a proactive, positive team player.

▶ A giant has a good reputation.

▶ A giant, like a general, needs to be built up with
responsibility and challenges.

▶ A giant can build and push up new giants.

Once a giant emerges, he can build, lead, and duplicate MDs
and builders. He can take charge and take care of his superteam. He can also help them grow into giants themselves.

"Giants are the ultimate system builders."

BUILDING STRATEGIES
THE CEO CLUB

In January 1997, we introduced A Plan to Focus. Its purpose was to create a recruiting explosion. Members were awarded a color coded shirt after reaching a certain level of recruiting numbers in their base.

THE CEO CLUB
A Plan to Focus

	Base Recruit Target		Actual Result
MONTH 1	10		
MONTH 2	15		
MONTH 3	25	Blue shirt	
MONTH 4	35		
MONTH 5	50	Pink shirt	
MONTH 6	50		
MONTH 7	50		
MONTH 8	75	Green shirt	
MONTH 9	75		
MONTH 10	100	Natural shirt	
MONTH 11	100		
MONTH 12	100		

SUPER BASE TARGETS

100 Recruits/ Month	200 Recruits/ Month	300 Recruits/ Month
Khaki shirt	Red shirt	Black shirt

The CEO Club created one of the biggest explosions in our team with powerful advantages:

1. A month-to-month focus teaching new members a recruiting mentality from the start.

2. A clear tracking and monitoring system for recruiting.

3. It unified recognition and motivated the team member to focus on large numbers of recruits, from double to triple digits.

Once the team member hit triple-digit levels, he had a good chance to run for CEO. Within that year we recruited a lot and produced a record number of CEOs.

The disadvantage was when people failed to move up to the next level of shirt recognition, they tended to give up trying.

Also, if the leader focused on recruiting for the sake of recruiting, he didn't provide good field training or match up field training to retain and build. The CEO Club worked to create recruiting momentum but was not strong on field training.

THE WEALTH BUILDER CHALLENGE

The Wealth Builder Challenge was introduced in 1998 to improve and compliment the CEO Club.

Using a pin system, team members were monitored and recognized by how many legs they built wide and deep (WD).

Build 3WD:
3 legs/Minimum Base 25K/mo

Build 6WD:
6 legs/Minimum Base 50K/mo

Build 9WD:
9 legs/Minimum Base 75K/mo

Build 12WD:
12 legs/Minimum Base or Superbase 100K/mo

Build 20WD:
20 legs/Minimum Superbase 500K/mo

Build 30WD:
30 legs/Minimum Superbase 1M/mo

The Wealth Builder Challenge encouraged a strong baseshop and superbase. It also aimed to increase width.

THE MD CLUB BUILDER PLAN

Begun in 2004 The MD Club Builder Plan initiated a new era for System Builders. The MD Club not only focused on recruiting but also a fast start to go deep and wide. It is the solution to building through duplicating.

This Is A Plan To Duplicate

THE MD CLUB		
A Plan to Duplicate		
	Target MD Clubs	Target MD Promotions
MONTH 1	1	
MONTH 2	2	
MONTH 3	2	Blue 5
MONTH 4	3	
MONTH 5	3	
MONTH 6	4	Red 15
MONTH 7	5	1
MONTH 8	5	1
MONTH 9	5	Gold 30	1
MONTH 10	5	1
MONTH 11	7	2
MONTH 12	8	Black 50	2
Total	*50 MD Clubs*	*8 MDs*

The MD Club so far has been working for more than 7 years. It continues to lay the groundwork for a new generation of System Builders using a clear, simple, doable system to fast start a new recruit into a building future.

3 – 3 – 30

"Can you recruit 3 and observe 3 complete PFS in 30 days?"

MEETINGS & EVENTS

*It's not about the meeting,
it's about the people who go to the meeting.
It's not about the teacher,
it's about the student.
It's not about the speaker,
it's about the listener.
And it's not about the convention,
it's about the convention's goals
that determine the success of the meeting.
But how successful it is
depends on you.*

THE MEETING FLOW

"A system whereby meetings and building never stop."

We Build People From Event To Event

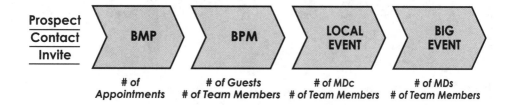

| Prospect / Contact / Invite | BMP | BPM | LOCAL EVENT | BIG EVENT |
| # of Appointments | # of Guests / # of Team Members | # of MDc / # of Team Members | # of MDs / # of Team Members |

Moving More People Faster

Our real business is to move people. It's unfortunate that most of us do not see the importance of the flow of moving people. Most new recruits don't go out in the field. Most team members don't go to the meeting. Many people don't participate in our local events. And worse quite a few miss the big event. If people don't move, nothing moves. Great builders understand it and master the art of moving and building people.

Great MDs And Builders Monitor These Numbers:

BMP: ▶ How many appointments the team has today

▶ How many trainees and trainers are out in the field

BPM: ▶ How many new guests attend

▶ How many team members show up

LOCAL EVENTS: ▶ How many team members attend monthly events

▶ How many new MD club members are promoted

▶ How many team members get recognized

BIG EVENT: ▶ How many members in the team / hierarchy attend

▶ How many MDs, new MDs, new leaders that rise up and take charge for their team in a big event

How A Big Builder Mind Is Being Built

Nobody can be built overnight. A big builder mind is built over countless field presentations, meetings, and events.

> BMP builds up your mind daily.
> BPM builds up your mind weekly.
> Local events build up your mind monthly.
> Big events build up your mind
> quarterly and yearly.

▶ A great builder knows that he must be in the field doing BMP every day. That's his habit, his business, his job. He learns to present, recruit, sell, make money, and train new people.

▶ But he must look forward to BPM twice a week to build up his vision, mission, and system. BPM is his baseshop day.

He starts to learn and build his team, to monitor and be monitored, and to run the system. A BPM impacts him the whole week.

▶ He also prepares for the big monthly events to develop new leaders and team members. He must fight for recognition as well as see his team rise up to the challenge. In terms of building a strong mindset, the local event collapses a month's worth of work into a single day.

▶ But it's the big event that changes lives. Team members may have slowed down for months or even years. But going to the big event can wake them up and move them back on the fast track overnight. It's like a year's worth of work compressed into one weekend.

How The Belief System Is Being Built

BMP	BPM	LOCAL EVENT	BIG EVENT
Believe in the Business	Believe in the System	Believe in Teamwork	Believe in Winning

When they believe in the business, they go out to BMP in the field every day.

When they believe in the system, they never miss the BPM.

When they believe in the team and in teamwork, they look forward to local events.

When they believe they can win, they want to change their life. They go to the big event no matter what.

"Small meetings build small people.
Big events build big builders."

BUILD PEOPLE FROM EVENT TO EVENT

From Small Meeting To Big Meeting:

Home Meeting

▶ Build relationships
▶ Get to know the family

Home BMP/BPM

▶ Recruit and invite

▶ Lead by example

▶ Foster duplication

▶ Create passion for the mission

▶ Sell the business to potential new prospects

> You can tell whether a person is serious about the business by watching him or her go to the BPM. Most people who show up Tuesday nights won't show up Saturday mornings.
> And unfortunately most people who show up Saturday mornings won't show up Tuesday nights. You can hardly find anybody who can go to both BPMs consistently.
> If you have one, then you have a potential builder.

Office BPM

▶ Sell the business to the team

▶ Recruit new people

Meeting After The Meeting - MD Club

▶ Manage team activities

▶ Be accountable for results

Fast Start

▶ Build a believer in the business

MD Club

▶ Monitor and build new MDs

▶ Learn to recruit and duplicate

Local Event

▶ Build future big basehop builders

MD Factory

▶ Build future big hierarchy builders

▶ Build a MD Factory

Big Event/Convention

▶ Stretch vision

▶ Bring the team to a higher level

▶ Fulfill major commitments

▶ Make key decisions

▶ Provide giant food for giants

*"Alone you cannot build people's minds.
But big events can."*

DON'T TRY TO CHANGE PEOPLE

During my career, I saw so many leaders trying to change people. Most of them sincerely believed that their job was to change people for the better.

As A Result, Most Leaders Tried Everything:

▶ More meetings

▶ More training

▶ More contests

▶ More motivation

▶ More counseling

▶ More coaching

These Efforts Have Some Influence, But Only A Little, Maybe 10%

"I believe 90% of change comes from inside the person, from a personal decision to change."

Most people won't change. Most people resist change. Most people won't change fast enough or significantly enough to help them win. That's why most people won't make it.

IF YOU CANNOT CHANGE YOUR PEOPLE, THEN CHANGE YOUR PEOPLE

The only thing you can do is to recruit more people into your organization and the ones who want to win will emerge.

Don't try to change people. It will only create agony and frustration for you. Just accept people the way they are.

Why It Is Nearly Impossible To Change Your People

You're not a prophet in your own land. Most of the time, your people will not listen to you, and if they do, they won't listen seriously. But when they go to the big event, they listen to other people.

Most people do not like to be told to change. They will change only from a personal decision deep inside of them and from somebody or something said that they can relate to.

"You cannot change people,
but you can bring people to life-changing events.
You cannot build people,
but you can bring people to big building events."

THE SIZE OF YOUR VISION

Can a pint size bottle hold a gallon of water?
Can a small minded person build it big?
You must have a bigger vision.
You must have a bigger container.
Be part of something bigger than yourself.
It will increase your vision.

GREAT EVENTS:
THE CHANGING MACHINE

*"You can never build a big team unless
you understand the importance of the big event."*

▶ At a big event, there is magic in crowds. The environment creates a condition for change.

▶ When people travel far away from home and spend time and money, they listen more seriously.

> **Small minds worship big people.**
>
> **Average minds worship big things.**
>
> **Great minds worship big events.**

▶ When the team travels together, they work with more intensity and urgency.

▶ People tend to compare themselves with others.

When they see someone just like them do it, they think, "If he can do it and if she can do it, then I can do it too."

*"There are people who tell us
there are too many meetings.
I think that's wonderful. The way I see it,
there should be many meetings
so that we have many chances to
change people's lives.*

THE MEETING BEFORE THE MEETING, THE MEETING AFTER THE MEETING

Just as the appetizer and the dessert could be as good as the main dish, the meeting before the meeting and the meeting after the meeting could be as important as the meeting itself.

Create A Meeting Mentality

Great system builders pay special attention to the meetings before and after the BPM, the BMP, and the big event.

As a great general with a powerful army never goes into battle without preparation, a great leader with a powerful team never goes into an event without a meeting before the meeting.

Moreover, the meeting after the meeting is the secret of a dominant team. Start strong, finish strong, and take the next step after an event.

Most successful builders meet before the BPM to prepare for the operation and meet after the BPM to capture and evaluate the results of their activities, just like most business owners who always come early to prepare for opening and always stay late to review the results of the day before closing.

> ▶ When taking teams to big events, the preparation, the briefing, and the mindset before entering the event ensures success during the event.
>
> ▶ The meeting after the event is also very critical because commitments and decisions will be made to elevate the team to the next level.

DON'T GET KILLED BY THE MEETING

Meetings are good. Meetings are our business. But too many meetings can hurt us.

I remember during my social worker career, it all started with a few meetings and some committees. But over time, I found myself going to meetings all day, all week long. Meetings at the city level, meetings at the county level, meetings at the state level, meetings at the federal level, meetings with different agencies, meetings with non-profit organizations, meetings with the neighborhood community, meetings with the business community, and meetings to bring all this information back to our staff.

One day I realized that the time we spend to service our clients is so little. Worse, by the time we get to our clients, it's usually too little, too late, and we're too exhausted.

"Meetings create more meetings, good or bad!"

There are many offices where the MDs and the leaders get bogged down with too many meetings and too much paperwork—meetings for the office, the task force, compliance, conference calls, etc.

REMEMBER: This is a business. You need to make money. And your people need to make money.

MAXIMIZE MEETINGS: Spend 90% of your time on activities with recruits and clients or anything related to recruits and sales.

MINIMIZE MEETINGS: Spend 10% of your time on activities related to paperwork and procedures or anything not related to recruits and sales.

BUILDING ON EXCITEMENT, BUILDING ON INSPIRATION

We have a lot of excitement, promotions, and contests. When business is slow and we want to crank up results, we tend to resort to some contest, trip, award, or promotion run, or we invite a motivational speaker to pump up our team.

Sometimes these fads may not be enough or provide lasting results. We need to look deep inside to see what truly inspires people.

EXCITEMENT	INSPIRATION
Recruit	Build
Make a sale	Help a family
Make money	Make a difference
Run for the title	Grow the team to the next level
Powerful speaker	Example of success
Outside	Inside
Short term	Long term

We need people to be excited. But if people are inspired, it is more genuine and long lasting. It's hard to have an outside speaker motivate while local leaders are not going out in the field and leading by example.

"Focus on inspiration, not motivation."

The Dynamics Of A Meeting

CHICAGO CONVENTION, 2002

We don't run the meeting. We create the meeting. We are one of the most dynamic forces in the financial services industry. Our meetings change all the time. Although we have a planning committee, we really just have a general feeling of what we want to do. So I know we're going to drive those guys in the industry crazy. But that's the way it is. There's a totally different animal sitting here. Even me, I don't know what I'm going to do in the meeting. But that ensures we have the best meeting.

MISSION

*The joy of life can't be
just good food, nice clothes,
fancy cars, and a happy family.
It includes the pain of defeat,
the hurt of endurance,
the fear of trying, the giving,
and the sacrifice for a cause
that benefits others.*

SELLING UNDERSTANDING VS SELLING THE PRODUCT

In the financial industry, there are many products and even more salespeople. Some spend all their lives selling term insurance. Some work for companies that sell only whole life. Others sell VUL or IUL. While still others specialize in nothing but annuities.

Many people jump into selling investment products when the stock market is hot, while others hawk mortgages when interest rates are low.

Companies spend a fortune developing new products, hiring new salespeople, and advertising to make products more appealing. Yet many people are still in a world of hurt. Lack of savings, mounting debt, and rising bankruptcy are the norms of today.

> You cannot see a doctor once and expect to stay healthy. The same is true with your car, which needs regular maintenance. Your financial situation is the same. It needs to be assessed on a regular basis.

Some people buy a variety of insurance products but lack savings and investments. Others have different kinds of savings and investments without understanding the need for protection. Still others get a new mortgage but may create more debt and more spending.

Quite often the person who sells insurance, investments, real estate, or mortgages hardly pays attention to other important aspects of their clients' financial needs. They also tend to see clients once and never come back to check up on them again. Very few people are willing to sit down on a regular basis to help people understand important concepts, how money works, their financial picture, and priorities of their future.

So it's not so much the product but the financial understanding that's most important. If people understand their needs, then they can buy the products that provide the solution.

> For example, when buying computers, many people buy hardware not knowing whether it suits their computing needs. But if they understand their software needs, they can buy the right hardware that will be up to the job.

A HIGHER LEVEL OF X-CURVE

"Don't sell a concept.
Sell a higher level of responsibility."

Take A Look At This Picture:

I often ask myself why some men barely have $100K protection and why some have $1 million or more. I'm also puzzled by how some people save $50 a month while others save $500 or more, even though both make about the same income.

Later on I realized that it depends on how these people view themselves. The man who has $100K protection sees himself worth $100K to his family versus the man who has $1 million protection sees himself worth $1 million if something were to happen to him. And the woman who saves $500 sees a wealthy future while the woman who saves $50 hardly seems to care about her family's future. I also believe the man who insures himself with $100K will probably see his future retirement at $100K. But the man who insures himself $1 million will expect to have millions in the future. Likewise, the parent who sets up an education plan for their children certainly sees that their children will go to college.

In our business, we are the luckiest people in the world because we understand our responsibility. Our mission is not to sell insurance and investments. Our mission is to educate people about sound financial concepts. If something were to happen to the breadwinner, we show families how to calculate their responsibilities and liabilities. We teach them how money works, how to pay themselves first, and how to build up their wealth.

Thus, don't sell them insurance. Don't sell them investments. Sell them a higher level of responsibility and a financially independent future. The responsible person will make good decisions for their family.

"Sell them a higher level of X Curve."

When a man is exposed to the right information and understands wealth building, they can change their life and their family life. If a man has a wealthy mind, eventually he can be wealthy. But a man who lacks a wealthy mind, even if he wins the lottery, will eventually be poor.

Our job is to plant the seed of wealth into people's minds and show them the way. Then they can complete the journey.

VISION OF A NEW INDUSTRY

This is the financial industry, but it's not. We just happen to be one of the best marketing, the most powerful, the most magnificent distribution systems in the world. Why do we want to be in this industry? This is one of the largest, most powerful, most important industries in the world.

THE OLD INDUSTRY	THE NEW INDUSTRY
Focus on sale	Focus on concept
Focus on product	Focus on solution
Focus on features & benefits	Focus on need & affordability
Focus on closing	Focus on understanding
Present the sale	Share information
One time deal	Regular checkup
Singular need	Overall picture
Customer	Client
Usually have quotas	No quotas
Commission	Mission
Recruit salespeople	Open outlets
Sell locally	Build and expand

HOW TO MAKE A SALE

"It's not about making a sale.
It's all about how you feel about what you do."

THE FOUR ELEMENTS OF MAKING A SALE:

▶ **Feel Good about Yourself**

▶ **Feel Good about Your Company and Your Product**

▶ **Give a Simple Presentation**

▶ **Let Them Make the Decision**

After a decade of going out in the field, I learned that unless I feel good about myself and about what I do, and unless I feel good about the company and the product I represent, everything else is useless.

Feel Good About Yourself, Your Company And Your Product

I share the challenges of many people. When I started the business, most of the people around me, my friends and my family, did not believe in me. That hurt my confidence, and I didn't feel too good about what I did.

In the early days, when I went out and made some money, I felt I did a good job. But deep down there was something that held me back.

Whenever I went to a party, and people asked me what I do, I'd always say I'm in financial services, although at the time I sold insurance. And when they asked me what kind of insurance I sell, I didn't even want to tell them. It took me a long time to say I sell life insurance.

In fact, many times I secretly wished that I failed. There was a part of me that thought it would just be easier to take a No than go on. I hoped that when I got to people's homes, they would tell me, "I'm busy. I can't see you." I would feel so good if they told me that. "I can go home now," I'd say to myself. "They're busy. It's not my fault." No wonder many people didn't buy from me.

But once in a while, when I felt strongly about what I did, when I was fired up after attending a great meeting, people bought from me and joined me. And the more I went out in the field, the more I realized that the things that held me back had nothing to do with the product or the marketplace. Rather, I was worrying too much about what other people thought about me.

I woke up to the fact that I don't just make a sale. I change people's lives. I help people take care of their families. I vowed to myself never to sell to people unless I felt strongly about my contribution.

From then on I went out in the field with pride. I knew that I was going to affect every family I talked to. Selling became less painful and less fearful. In fact, I began to like it. Now, I love to talk to people. I love to share with them what I know. And that has made all the difference.

Give A Simple Presentation

Keep it simple. Don't overload people with facts and figures. It's important that people understand the financial concepts and what our services and products can do for them. Make sure people understand the benefits as well as the costs. Make sure it's good for them.

Time yourself. People don't have the whole night to listen.

> **REMEMBER:**
> Most clients do not have the sophisticated knowledge that you have.
>
> How much you know does not matter.
>
> What matters is how much they understand.

Let Them Make The Decision

A few years into the business, one night, all of a sudden, I got enlightened. I figured out the secret of closing a sale.

"The real secret to making a sale: There is no secret."

People Make Up Their Own Minds

▶ Those people who want to buy—they will buy.

▶ Those people who don't want to buy—no matter what— they won't buy.

After that realization, every night when I went out in the field and talked to people, I knew whether or not a client wanted to buy. My sixth sense told me that the person who wants to buy will give me a check and the person who doesn't won't.

So if you want to have a great closing ratio, sell only to the person who wants to buy. And if the person doesn't want to buy, don't sell to him.

> *"You don't make a sale.*
> *You share important information that*
> *may help change people's lives."*

THE BEST SALESMAN IN THE WORLD

"You can be the best salesman in the world."

Did you know that I am the best salesman in the world? Yes, that's right. I am. As far as I know, nobody is better than me. I have a 100% closing ratio. Not 99%. Not 99.9%. But 100%. Isn't that incredible?

Did you know that I am also the best recruiter in the world? I can't fail. My recruiting ratio is also 100%. Isn't that unbelievable?

Did you know that I am also the best builder in the world? Everyone I build, 100% of them become MD, CEO, or a giant builder. Isn't that powerful?

Let me tell you my secret.

Every time I go out to make a sale, I present, take information, make recommendations, and offer solutions to families. I want to make sure they understand and are happy with what I show them.

Then I will ask them their decision. If they want to buy, then I will sell to them. If they don't want to buy or are not so sure, I won't sell to them. I tell them, "I only sell to the person who wants to buy." If they don't want to buy, if they're not sure… well, I don't want to sell to them because it will affect my record. That's how I have a 100% closing ratio.

Every time I recruit someone, I show them the opportunity. I share with them information about our business. I let them know the good as well as the bad, the challenges as well as the rewards. Then I will ask them for their decision. If they are not so sure, I will not recruit them. I tell these men and women, I don't want you to mess up my record. Again, "I recruit 100% of the people who want to join."

Every time I sit down with a team member, I tell them what they need to do to become successful. I tell them about the hard work, the sacrifices, the price they must pay, and the commitment they have to make. If they are not committed, if they are not willing to keep trying until they reach their goal, I won't commit to them. That's how I have a 100% record to build.

Now you know my secret: "I sell to the person who wants to buy, recruit the person who wants to join, and build the person who wants to build."

Some of you may find it funny, but I take it quite seriously. In fact, this secret saved my career. I see many people in our business try to sell to the person who doesn't want to buy. They keep recruiting the person who doesn't want to join. And worst of all, they constantly chase after the person who doesn't want to build. This will eventually kill them. It eats them up every day. Their lives become filled with misery and frustration.

Every time people don't buy, they blame themselves. They're not good enough. They don't have enough training. And every time people say No, they feel hurt. They don't understand why their friends and relatives won't join them. They blame the trainer or the office environment. And every time their team members don't go to the field, don't attend the meeting, don't produce, or aren't successful, they mull over all the same problems. They are desperate to find the way to motivate the person who doesn't want to be motivated. They think that they have a poor closing ratio and an awful building record.

Remember: You can only recruit the person who wants to join, sell to the person who wants to buy, and build the person who wants to build. That will give you peace of mind to move on, and you will be successful because there are so many people out there who need your help. Thousands of people want to change their lives, thousands want to be financially independent, and thousands of our teammates want to win.

"Some will. Some won't. So what?"

SELLING: DIFFICULT OR EASY?

"It's up to you."

To many people, selling is probably one of the most difficult things in the world. That's how I felt early on. But as time passed, I found out it's not as hard as I thought.

1. People Are Different

Some people are difficult, some people are easy, and some people who seem to be difficult at first actually turn out to be not that difficult at all.

2. I Can't Sell

Most of us think that you have to be a slick salesperson for people to buy. Nothing is further from the truth. Actually most clients like to see the sincere belief and conviction in you. You will be surprised by the number of people who will buy from you. During my first few years, I always wondered why people bought from me despite the fact that my presentation skills were not so good.

3. You Have No Quotas

You're in business for yourself. Nobody forces you to sell. You have no quotas. You have no pressure. Most of the time, you're part-time, you have a job, and you have other sources of income. Whether or not you make a sale, it won't make or break you.

4. It's Not A Job

It's not a job. You're not an employee of a sales force. You do this because you like it. You want to do it. You love going out in the field and helping people. So if you love what you do, and if you believe in what you do, it's not that difficult, is it?

5. You Look For The Believers

Most of the time, while sharing the concepts and products, you don't just make a sale. Your potential client could be a potential recruit who believes in what we do and may join us to go out and share our mission.

6. It's A Numbers Business

Ultimately, it's a numbers business. There are good days. There are bad days. If you see more people, you have more chances. In this world, when someone is selling something, somebody is buying something.

7. It Only Seems Difficult At First

After your first 3 or 4 sales, you will begin to feel good. After 15 to 20 sales, you will feel great. After 30 to 40 sales, you are in business. Just like anything in life, success breeds more success.

NEVER TRY TO BE A SALESPERSON

I'm not sure this is the right approach or the right thinking, but in the last 26 years of being in the "sales business," I never thought of myself as a salesperson, nor have I wanted to be particularly good in sales.

I have nothing against selling, a sales career, or salespeople. In fact, I'm quite good at making the sale. I made good money most of my career through personal sales, training sales, and referral sales.

I also believe that if you're not a good personal producer, it will be hard for you to become a good trainer, and, therefore, it will be more difficult for you to be a big basehop and hierarchy builder.

That said, I have a strong belief that if you have a good product and you bring real value to the client, you don't need to be a good salesperson. The same goes with recruiting. If you offer a legitimate opportunity, you don't need to be a good recruiter.

"You just sell to the person who wants to buy and recruit the person who wants to join."

A System Builder Will Bring Out Better Results And More Sales Than A Salesperson

Normal salespeople sell products. System builders sell the system, opening the outlets that will move products on a much bigger scale.

I like to make a sale. But I love to do training sales. During training sales, I get to make the sale as well as train the future trainers of my organization. I also don't want to be too good, too "professional", or too slick in sales, because my people cannot duplicate it. I'd rather make a simple sale that can be duplicated rather than make a sophisticated, non-duplicatable sale.

> *"Salespeople pay attention*
> *to the close of the sale.*
> *Builders pay attention to the mission,*
> *the crusade of the sale,*
> *and the education of the trainee*
> *during the sales process."*

Thus, if you make a complicated sale, a nagging sale or a lengthy sale, even if you get the sale, you lose the trainee.

> Sometimes, the best sale you make is the one you don't make. Have the courage and will to walk out of a difficult or inappropriate situation. Even if you do not make the sale, you may actually make the best impression on your trainee.

SELLING TO YOUR DOWNLINE

"The most important sale is the sale to your recruit or your downline."

Your downline must know the reason why they buy—not because they're your downline and not because they joined.

They buy because they recognize how good the products are for their family and for their needs. They must understand the concept and know their financial situation and their goal. They believe in our mission. They see our crusade, what we do to help people.

We don't want a sale. We want an inspiration.

They must see the benefits, feel great about the sales process, and be proud about the transaction.

The secret of your success is not because you're a good salesperson. It's because you do it right. You do it with pride. Your recruit will remember their first sale for the rest of their life.

YOUR CLIENTS ARE MORE THAN JUST A SALE

"Build a large base of multi-product-using clients."

1. Keep A List Of All Your Clients

Not only do you need a large base of recruits, you also need to retain a large base of clients who may want and need multiple products.

2. Call And Visit Your Clients And Ask For Referrals

Satisfied clients give the best referrals. Your clients will have new friends and acquaintances whom they could refer you to.

3. Clients Need Regular Financial Health Check Ups

Your clients appreciate it when you check in from time to time. They may need some adjustment or additional coverage to their policy. They may need to start a college fund for their new child or find out about more ways to invest their money.

4. Recruit Your Clients

Timing is everything. The client who wasn't interested a year ago might be interested today. Most clients or their spouses do have some degree of interest in our business. At the very least, they are already convinced about the products and concepts. All you have to do is talk about the opportunity. It is just a matter of time.

WHY PEOPLE DON'T BUY

Two Main Reasons:
1. They don't understand.
2. They don't believe you.

When people don't understand the concept or the product, they will not make a decision. Make sure to ask them if there is anything they do not understand. Also, people don't buy because either they don't believe you or they don't trust you.

▶ So be sincere. Tell it like it is. Show them the advantages as well as the disadvantages.

▶ If you can afford not to make a sale, you can make a sale. The times when you want to make a sale so badly are the times when you can't make a sale.

The Hidden Reasons

Many times, when I thought I had an obvious sale, I could never close. This drove me crazy. Later on, I found out that there were so many hidden reasons. The clients' marriage was in chaos. They were in financial trouble. One of them had serious health problems. And many other reasons. But of course, they wouldn't disclose that information to me.

This realization reduced my frustration and saved my career. I thought that there was something wrong with me or something wrong with my presentation. Maybe it was the way I talked, or maybe I was not excited enough.

Now, the way I see it, if they don't buy, they don't buy. All I can do is give them my best effort. It's their life. It's their decision.

When a friend or relative doesn't buy, many of us tend to take it personally. Relax. They'll buy someday. And even if they don't, your career cannot rely solely on a handful of friends or relatives anyway. If you're a real estate broker and bank your career on your circle of friends and relatives, your career won't last too long. You don't open a restaurant on that basis either. It's business, my friend.

> *Imagine you own a clothing store, and someone walks in, looks interested in a shirt, and tries it on, but doesn't buy it. Don't knock your head against the wall trying to figure out why the person didn't buy.*

SELL ONLY TO THE PERSON WHO REALLY WANTS TO BUY

In my career there have always been friends and relatives who say, "Since you're my relative/friend, I will buy from you."

This seems good, but it's not. I would tell them, "No, don't do me any favors. I want you to buy only if you need it and because it benefits your family. Then I would appreciate you a lot more!"

"Easy come, easy go.
Most easy sales are easily canceled!"

▶ If they do you a favor, later on, when they meet other friends or relatives who sell similar things, they may cancel your policy and do the other friend or relative a favor. I've seen many clients change their policies or investments because a close friend or relative told them to.

▶ If they do you a favor and buy, in the long term, they won't feel good about it, even if they keep it. And of course, you will feel like you owe them, which is not good either.

▶ If they buy from you as a favor, they won't recommend you or the product to others. You may miss the opportunity to serve many other families.

We do people a favor by educating them. Our job is not to make a sale. Our purpose is to help people take charge of their financial future. Thus, when they decide to buy, they must know exactly what they're getting into.

This is not a shirt or a pair of shoes. This is a long-term commitment that requires a lot of discipline. If they don't understand the product and concepts, they won't keep the product long term. In the end, it serves no one if they cancel early.

We don't do anybody a service when people cancel. If we convince people to buy, and they cancel, they may lose money, and that's even worse than if they didn't buy.

So please, don't do me any favors!

> **REMEMBER:**
> When selling to good friends or relatives, make sure both husband and wife listen and understand. Don't take any short cuts. The same holds true for recruiting. Don't recruit anyone who is only doing you a favor.

A NEW CONCEPT
IN THE COMPENSATION SYSTEM

*"I'd rather have 1% of 100 people's efforts
than 100% of my own effort."*
— J. PAUL GETTY

How do you explain the difference between a system based on sales and one based on building? Most of the industry out there normally don't recruit or build. We do. We focus on building a large network of outlets, a large number of licensed team members.

Traditional Commission vs Spread And Overrides

In the following illustrations, note that Mr. A, Mr. B, and everyone under Mr. B are fully licensed. The three examples are simply hypothetical scenarios intended to help illustrate the concept of spread and overrides. This is a conceptual description, not the actual spread of this company or any company.

As you can see, in the first example, we split 100% of the commission into 80% and 20%. Thus, if Mr. B makes a sale, he earns only 80%, but he recruits 5 people and builds them. So, if tonight Mr. A makes 1 sale, he would make 100% of the commission. But if Mr. B and his 5 people each make 1 sale, Mr. B would earn 180% in commissions—80% from his own sale and 100% from 20% overrides of 5 people's sales.

In the second example, if Mr. A makes 1 sale, he still earns 100%. But if Mr. B makes 1 sale, and each of his 1st and 2nd generation makes 1 sale, he overrides 2 levels now,

A Conceptual Explanation of Spread and Overrides

Sale: Focus on high personal contract   **Building:** Focus on many levels of override/spread

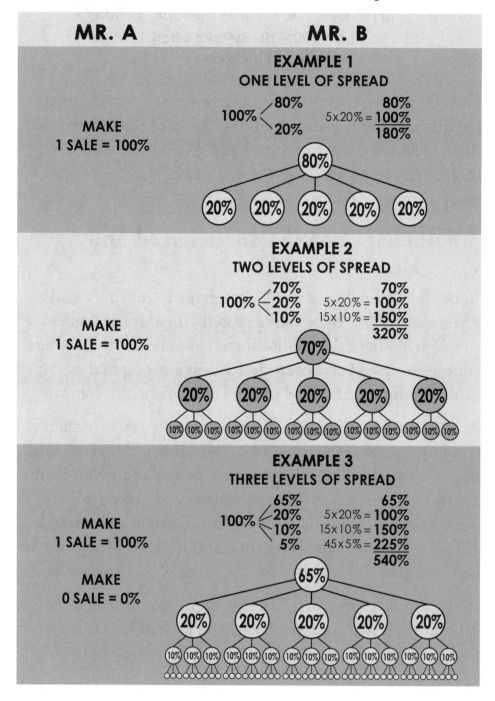

totaling 320%. In the 3rd example, Mr. A still makes 100% from 1 sale, but Mr. B makes 540% from 3 levels of overrides, assuming each person under Mr. B makes 1 sale.

In these examples, by reducing the personal contract of Mr. B from 80% down to 70% and again down to 65%, we create more levels of overrides, or more spread.

Please note that in the building system, Mr. B has many people working with him and for him. Mr. A doesn't. So while Mr. A will make 0% if he doesn't make a sale, if Mr. B doesn't sell or can't make a sale, he can still make money on overrides—100% in example 1, 250% in example 2, and 475% in example 3.

However, in the building system, if Mr. B fails to recruit or build, he won't have people working with him and for him. Or if Mr. B does have people but they don't perform, Mr. B can only make 80%, 70%, or 65%, depending on his contract, through personal sales.

That's why in our system it's so crucial to recruit and build a large number of people. Only then can there be people making sales for you.

"The person who recruits the most makes the most."

THE TRAINER

"Field trainer is one of the best jobs in the world."

Field trainer is probably the best kept secret in the financial industry. This is one of the greatest jobs you can dream of.

1. YOU TEACH PEOPLE: Give someone a fish, and he'll eat for a day. Teach someone how to fish, and it will change their life forever.

2. EASIER SALE: When the trainee takes you to their warm market—to meet their friend, relative, coworker or neighbor—it's a salesperson's paradise.

3. EASIER TO RECRUIT: The same thing happens with recruits. Their recruit is your recruit. You have a cheerleader rooting for you.

4. UNLIMITED MARKET: Every trainee brings you their natural market. And these prospects bring you even more recruits. And sales from those recruits generate more referrals. So as long as you want to train, you won't run out of places to go.

5. A WIN-WIN SITUATION: You train and duplicate new builders. The trainee builds their team. You make money. The trainee learns. A consumer gets helped. A potential prospect is offered a chance.

6. TRAINING IS BUILDING: Trainers are builders. Great builders are great trainers. Why should you look for personal sales when you could make the training sale? The training sale is the stone that kills two birds. You get the sale, and at the same time the trainee gets trained.

Every time you train to make a sale, you get paid more than just making a sale. In fact, you begin a process of sales multiplication. It's like a farmer planting seed. When you train a person, it's like adding water and fertilizer to your crops. Soon, when your trainee becomes a trainer, your tree begins to bear fruit.

Remember: Every time you train to recruit, you get more than just a new recruit. You are always one recruit away from an explosion. This could be the one.

7. TRAINING IS DUPLICATING: People will duplicate you, good and bad, especially the new trainee. Their early experience in the field will affect them tremendously for the rest of their career. You can make or break a future, so be extremely careful. Thus, the four ingredients of duplication must be strictly observed: simple, clear, fast, and easy.

In addition, it's not your skill or aptitude but rather your spirit and attitude that matter most. You must inject four positive images of a system builder: honest, respectful, mission-driven, and enthusiastic.

"Be a good trainer.
Be a great master copy."

> **BUILDER'S NOTE:**
>
> Make sure to be on time for the appointment.
>
> Always call ahead if you are late and please answer your phone.

TEAM BUILDING

The Ladder of Evolution
From nobody to
UPSTART
From upstart to
CONTENDER
From contender to
WINNER
From winner to
CHAMPION
From champion to
DYNASTY

– PAT RILEY

TEAMWORK MAKES THE DREAM WORK

"TEAM: Together Everyone Achieves More"

The purpose of a team is to win and to win bigger than any individual could. A team needs team players, and they must expect that they and their team will win.

Here, we are in business for ourselves but not by ourselves.

BE PART OF THE TEAM: Many people in the team building business want to build a team but can't be team players themselves. It's not I, me, mine. It's we, us, ours. Put the team first.

TRUST: When there is doubt about and lack of trust among members, there will be no team and the individual won't engage. Give people a chance. Give

> *A fool is the person who trusts everyone but also the person who trusts no one.*

people the benefit of the doubt. Give your leader, your trainer, and your team a chance to work with you.

COMMIT TO A MISSION: Without a shared goal, we don't have a team. Our team is committed to the mission of making a difference for families.

FIGHT TO WIN: You work as an individual, but you fight as a team. Teamwork gives you more strength and courage to win. When the team wins, you also win.

BUILD THE TEAM: When you're in the team, so are your teammates. Together everyone can build a team naturally.

TEAM SPIRIT: In the team business, moody people are not very good for the team. Team members need to be positive, upbeat, and coachable. They need to stumble forward, lead by example, and persevere.

Helping others is also at the heart of being a team player. Thus, in our business, not only our teammates but also our clients benefit from this spirit.

DREAMWORK: Through a large number of people who join hands for a common goal, everyone can win. Teamwork is dreamwork. It can make your dreams come true.

COMPETITION: THE NATURE OF THE TEAM

"A team that does not compete is a team that lacks purpose and unity."

In the team business, you need to recognize that the very nature of the team is to compete. Without competition, there is no game, no team to compete with.

There are many people who think that this is a sales organization or a financial services business. "Why bother with competition and recognition?" they say. There are quite a few who are even more blunt: "Don't bother with the plaque. Just send me the check!"

You need to open up and work with others. An isolated team will be suffocated with boredom and have no momentum.

You can be a loner with that attitude, but you won't make it in a team. You can't build a team without having your team-mates compete with each other and with other teams.

You need to bring your team to the big event. The big event is like the Super Bowl, the ultimate arena of competition.

"Every time we compete or run for a goal, a promotion, or a challenge, the team rises up to a new level and new stars are born."

Teams grow with competition. Competition builds and tests leaders. You will find out how people perform under pressure, how they play when they're hurt.

"Your job as a coach and as a leader is to talk about winning all the time."

TEAM = PEOPLE + CARE

Anytime I see an office, a baseshop, or a hierarchy in bad shape, I look for the missing element: care.

MOST OF THE TIME THE CAUSE OF THE PROBLEM LIES AMONG 10 REASONS:

1. The leader cares less about his business.

2. The leader is distracted.

3. The leader begins to cool down.

4. The leader cares less about what's going on with the team.

5. The leader lacks communication.

6. The leader lacks overlapping leadership.

7. The leader cares little whether their team wins or not.

8. The team members are selfishly shielding.

9. The team members do not volunteer or respond to the upline's challenges.

10. Each leg in the team cannot work and cooperate together.

Like a sports team, if each player in the organization does not care for each other and does not care to win, you don't have a team.

A lot of people work for money, but that's not necessarily the most important thing to them. Rather, it's the team that they're working with and the leader that they follow which both play a big part in their performance.

"People don't care about how much you know.
They just want to know how much you care."

> Every night, there are people in your team who stay awake and think about you.
> They probably ponder 3 things:
> - ▶ Your Integrity
> - ▶ Your Commitment
> - ▶ If You Care About Them

SYSTEM BUILDER AND SYSTEM USER

SYSTEM BUILDER	SYSTEM USER
■ Work for the team	◆ The team works for him
■ Do it first	◆ Tell team to do it first
■ Focus on mission	◆ Focus on override
■ Work more than talk	◆ Talk more than work
■ Come early, stay late	◆ Come late, leave early
■ Volunteer on teamwork, meeting, conventions	◆ Often have excuses on teamwork, conventions
■ Leading	◆ Misleading
■ Tend to be silent contributor	◆ Quite vocal, good on being demanding
■ Don't take credit	◆ Take more credit than is deserved
■ Giver	◆ Taker

Although it appears clear who is who, can you tell who is the system builder and who is the system user? In reality, the difference is not so easy to tell. Anywhere in our society, there are those who build and contribute, and there are those who use and abuse.

*"Be a system builder.
Be proud to be a system builder."*

FOLLOW YOUR UPLINE, FOLLOW YOUR DOWNLINE, FOLLOW YOUR SIDELINE

"If the blind lead the blind, both shall fall in the ditch."
— MATTHEW 15:14

Who should you follow? Should you follow your upline? Your upline has more experience, but what if your upline is on the wrong path? Should you follow your downline? Your downline is the source for potential recruits and production, but what if your downline is not moving? Should you follow your sideline? They're part of the office, but what if they have a different way of doing things?

> *"Follow your upline, and you may go up.*
> *Follow your downline, and you may go down.*
> *Follow your sideline,*
> *and you may go around and around."*

It's incredible how people slow down or get negatively influenced because of the people around them. Students get poor grades or sidetracked. Employees get lost, confused, and frustrated in their jobs. The same is true with people in this business. Instead of following success, pursuing their dream, submitting to the proven system, and aligning with successful builders, they tend to look around, research more, and analyze every single issue. It doesn't take long to get them confused and frustrated before they lose their dream.

"Follow the truth. Follow your heart. Follow your dream."

TOO LOYAL

*"Silence in the face of injustice makes
a coward out of man."*

— ABRAHAM LINCOLN

I watched a movie recently about a family. The husband is
a really bad guy. He beats his wife, but every time he abuses
her, he comes up with lies to make up with her, so she's happy
again. Then he abuses his child. The child tells her mother. He
denies everything, and she believes him. Then he abuses the
child again. The child complains, and the mother gets mad.
He apologizes and says he won't do it again. The story goes on.

Throughout my life, I saw it
all around me. Many people
all over the world are loyal to
their partners, many people
are loyal to their family, many
subordinates are loyal to their
boss—in spite of frequent injus-
tices done to them or to others.

> *It's not a movie.
> It's life.*
>
> *Most people are
> very loyal. Loyalty
> is a great virtue,
> but it can easily
> be abused.*

It's the issue of integrity versus
loyalty. Which one comes first?

How loyal are you to your parents if they're wrong? How loyal
are you to your leader if he no longer follows the successful
path? What about the downline? What about your business?

Don't get me wrong. This is not meant to create any conflict.
I just don't want you to let the distracted upline who is slowing down hurt your business. I want you and your people to
have the courage to stay on track to your dreams.

THE SHIELDING EFFECT

"Cover the grass from sunshine, and it will die."

Shielding happens when an upline decides to shield his downline or his team from a higher upline.

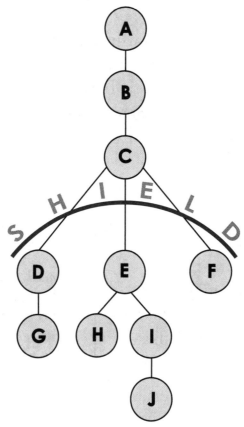

C is the "shielder". C shields his team from A and B.

D, E, F, G, H, I, J are the "shieldees".

There are so many reasons why people shield. Here are the most popular:

1. DOESN'T LIKE THE UPLINE: Somehow C doesn't get along with or simply doesn't like B or A.

2. WAITS FOR LICENSE: C is greedy.

3. EGO: They may not want the team exposed to more knowledgeable, more powerful, and more successful leaders.

4. SELFISH: They treat people like toys. "My team belongs to me!"

5. AFRAID OF LOSING INFLUENCE: They want everyone under their control.

6. LAZY: They are afraid of being asked for bigger numbers or for more commitment.

7. HATES MEETINGS AND EVENTS: "If I don't go, you don't go."

8. INSECURE: Believe it or not, some are even afraid the downline may perform better than them and surpass them.

9. AND TONS OF OTHER REASONS...

EXCEPTION:
In some rare instances, when A and B are really the bad guys, it is justified for C to protect his team from negative influences. The problem is, who's to judge whether A and B are good or bad? What about C? Is C good or bad? Well, nobody really knows who's the bad guy, and nobody would admit that either, especially the bad guy!

So Who's To Blame?

The shielder, C? Yes, C's the one.

The shieldees, D, E, F, G, H, I, and J? Yes, they are blameworthy as well.

Why? Because they let C do it to them! They're independent businesspeople. Nobody can control them unless they allow it. So please do not act like a victim if this ever happens to you.

Most often the end result of a shielding situation is a dead team or, at best, a struggling one.

"Shielding is a no-win situation!"

ALIGNMENT

"Without alignment, a car can't run fast."

Alignment is often misinterpreted as "follow the leader, follow the upline". But what if the upline is not aligned? In a convoy, what if the car in front of you stears toward the wrong direction?

You should be aligned only if the car in front of you follows the path of success.

OVERLAPPING LEADERSHIP

GREAT BUILDERS' RULES OF ENGAGEMENT
Rule 1: Every recruit in the base is your direct.
Rule 2: Every MD in the hierarchy is your first.

Most MDs and trainers make the fatal mistake of only taking care of their own recruits while letting other team members take care of their recruits' recruits. It's only okay if those other leaders are capable. In reality, though, that's not always the case. Many are not good trainers. Many don't even take their people out in the field. It's like a mother asking her teenage son to take care of the 10 year old, and the 10 year old to take care of the 5 year old, and the 5 year old to take care of the new born baby. It doesn't work that way in life. It should not work that way in our business.

The MD must know and take care of everyone in the base. She must treat everyone like her direct recruit. She should get to know them, talk to them, set their goals, communicate and follow up with everyone on a daily basis.

The same thing applies with a big hierarchy. The big builder must know, work with, and always be accessible to all MDs in the team, regardless of generation. She cannot expect a non-MD to build a MD. Nor can she hope for a non-WSB to build a WSB.

Thus, the MD must take full responsibility to help everyone in her base become MD. Likewise, the WSB must overlap leadership to help every MD in her hierarchy become WSB. This will provide peace of mind and an equal chance for everyone in the team to receive all the guidance, leadership, and coaching they need to become a big builder.

"You must overlap to build it big."

LEADER OR BUILDER

Leadership is everything. But in our business, leadership alone may not be enough. There is often a misunderstanding about the role of a leader versus that of a builder.

It's interesting that many people prefer to be a leader rather than a builder. When they have people under them, they want to lead so badly that they forget they really need to be a builder first. They develop "leadership" skills like public speaking, teaching, and motivating instead of doing, field training, duplicating, and showing results. They get so good and so slick, so sophisticated and complicated, that one day they're no longer duplicatable.

There are areas in life that need leaders. But in a system where duplication is key, builders are needed. In big systematized enterprises like Wal Mart, Starbuck's, McDonald's, or Home Depot, you don't really hear a lot about their leaders, but you know they have a lot of silent builders.

BUILDER'S TRAP:
After hitting the MD position, many people fall into this trap and slow down their building efforts significantly.

BUILDERS ARE NOT PROBLEM SOLVERS

In the people business, you deal with lots of people. Every one of them is different. They have different ideas, opinions, situations, challenges, and a lot of problems.

How To Deal With These Problems?

Don't. Except for a handful of serious issues related to the business, the large majority of people's problems are a waste of time.

If you stay in this business long enough, you'll be amazed by the amount of problems people have or create for themselves and then bring to you.

When people go to work at a job, they seem to mention no problems. Yet when people come into our business, they will have an endless list of problems: "I have no time... My car broke down... I have babysitting challenges... My spouse is not happy... I have other things to do first..."

> So many people would love to bring you their problems, as long as you're willing to hear them.

They never say any of this to their boss.

On the job, if you show up, they pay. If you don't show up, they won't pay, or they fire you. They don't need to know about your problems.

▶ You can't solve family problems. For most couples, the problems of their relationship existed before they joined the business.

▶ You can't loan people money. First, you can never have enough money to loan to everybody. Second, you often just delay a bigger problem.

▶ You can't recruit for them. They have to prospect, go out, stay motivated, and do what is necessary to hit their goal.

▶ You can't sell for them. They have to go out in the field, get referrals, and learn to sell on their own initiative.

▶ You can assist. You can support them up to a certain point. But you can't do their job.

▶ People need to overcome their own problems. They need to talk to and get support from their own families. They need to reorganize their life for their business, to do what's important for them and their families.

"You're not a problem solver!"

REMEMBER:

You're a leader. You're NOT a marriage counselor. You're NOT a psychiatrist. You're NOT a banker. You're NOT a social worker. You're NOT a taxi driver. You're NOT a babysitter. You're a builder.

NEVER GIVE UP

HOUSTON CONVENTION, 2002

The whole nature of our business is to do something we thought was impossible. That's why we get together to draw on each other's energy and unleash the giant power inside us.

I could not do what I did today had I not believed in myself and my people. I could never build a big team if I didn't believe deadly in every single one of you.

The reason I stick with people through thick and thin—even the worst guy, and I never leave them no matter what—is because I know they're going to win. I'm willing to spend night after night and week after week and fly across the country because I know they're going to win.

Hey people, you cannot take shortcuts.

The reason you lose is because you give up too quickly on your people. But do you know what's the real reason? You give up on you. Most of you give up on you. It reflects from inside you to the outside. If you know you're going to win anyway, you never give up on anybody else.

I'm not trying to criticize anybody. There were times in my career when I slowed down too. I'm not a superman. There were times I wanted to give up on people too. There were times I wanted to give up on myself. I wanted to throw in the towel everyday. Everyday in the last 26 years I asked myself, "Should I slow down tomorrow?"

Quitting is not an option, but slowing down is always an option, which is equal to quitting for me. You don't have to completely quit. You just quit trying.

I only have one chance right now in my life, and the older I am the more I feel how precious my life is. I think about the time I live on this earth. Life is too short. Click, you're thirty years old. Click, next thing you're forty. Click, you're fifty. And I hate the next click.

Please don't give up on yourself. And please believe in your people. And if you don't believe in yourself, why are you here? You expect people to follow people like you, who always doubt yourself, always shaky?

If you don't believe in our people and our mission, why are you here? I think the guy who collects over-rides and disappears at least has some integrity. At least he says to the whole world, "You know what? I just want the money." At least he declares his intentions publicly.

You cannot be a leader and tell people to follow you if you act like a wimp. You're killing people! You cannot allow yourself to be weak. When you take people to follow you, you have to be strong.

This is a fight. You don't have to have big numbers to say you're winning. You win when you have small numbers! You win best when you're down! I don't care if you do 5K or 10K in your base. But you act like a winner! You act like a leader! Then, you lead people.

The smaller numbers you have, the stronger you should be to your team. The bigger the trap you're in, the stronger you should be to your team, because at the worst of times your people look up to you. Imagine you're captain of a ship and when you get lost, you don't know what to do. During the worst of times, that's when the team needs you most.

Most of you dance like kings when you have big numbers. But when you have small numbers, you want to make the whole world feel bad. "I'm hurting. I don't have money." Grow up. It's hard to ask people to believe in you when you don't even believe in yourself.

Rise up! Stand up! You always have a chance. Things can change tomorrow. We're in business to change. And we're in business to win. Any army, any team, at the most crucial time, when you're down, when you hit the bottom, and you call the right shot, you rise up, the hero rises up, and you change the whole game! In the battlefield or the playing field, when it's the darkest of hours, at the weakest point, somebody rises up and changes the whole thing because somebody believed in himself and believed in the destiny of the team!

> ## *ANATOMY OF AN EXPLOSION*
> ### Conditions for Ignition:
>
> 1. *A High Level of Frustration*
>
> 2. *An Unusual Surge in the Attitude of Leaders*
>
> 3. *A Big Dream Written Down in a Specific Plan*
>
> 4. *A Mastermind Alliance of Key Leaders*
>
> 5. *A Daring Action / A Bold Move*

WINNING MINDSET

Happiness

is helping

a friend become

financially

independent.

TAKE CHARGE OF YOUR BUSINESS

"God gets you to the plate, but once you're there, you're on your own."
— TED WILLIAMS

It puzzles me that there are so many dependent people who want to be financially independent. They never seem to know anything. Their favorite words are "Where?" "How?" and "Why?"

Many of these people have been in the business a long time, yet they act as if they joined yesterday. They look like the husband who goes into the kitchen and keeps asking his wife, "Where are the forks? How do I turn on the stove? Why won't the dishwasher work?"

> *"Where is the class? Where are the forms? Where is the school? Where is the meeting?" "How do I recruit? How do I sell? How do I use the computer?" "Why won't anybody teach me? Why didn't anybody tell me? Why does this happen?"*

When they go to conventions, they always let the upline book the room, rent the car, chauffeur them around, and even wake them up. A leader once said, "My business is running a giant adult day care!" Everybody admittedly laughed. Ironically, when these same people go on their own vacation, they plan and do everything—buy tickets, book the room, rent the car—without any problem.

"It's a shame to be in a business of personal growth and never grow up!"

How can you ever become a leader if you keep letting people take care of you, remind you, and motivate you all the time?

Why don't you book your own room, rent your own car, and find your own way? Why don't you take charge of your business? Why don't you step up and become a servant leader?

It's not your upline's business. It's not your downline's business. It's not your sideline's business. It's not the company's business. It's your business.

"You need to be independent before you can achieve financial independence."

One day, a team member asked me to teach him the features of a new product.

My reply: "We are both licensed. We are both businesspeople. This is a new product. How can you expect me to learn and teach you? Here is the brochure, the prospectus, and the forms.

I have to read, learn, and understand the same product for my business.

I never expect anybody to learn for me. Why don't you do the same for your business?"

FOR REAL BUSINESS 7-POINT TEST

1. Daily activities
2. Results
3. Meetings
4. Duplicate new builders
5. Prospecting
6. Systematized
7. Business mindset

Rate Yourself On These 7-Point Tests

1. DAILY ACTIVITIES: Are you going out in the field everyday? How many appointments of BMP, PFS, prospecting, recruiting, sales, stop by, drop by do you have? You should have 2 to 5 for real appointments every day.

2. RESULTS: Do you have results? If you have appointments but no results, are these appointments for real? You should have 2 to 5 recruits or sales per week.

3. MEETINGS: Do you attend all meetings and events? Do you understand the importance of the meeting?

4. DUPLICATE NEW BUILDERS: After all the sales, the recruits and the meetings, what good is it if you build no builders?

You should build 2 to 5 new MD Club members and trainers every month.

5. PROSPECTING: The hardest test is this one. Do you still prospect every day and add new names to your PPL? How many personal recruits do you have this month?

6. SYSTEMATIZE: How systematized are you? Do you believe in the system? Do you follow the system?

7. BUSINESS MINDSET: Do you put time and money in the business? How many hours do you put in as a part-time associate or as a full-timer? Do you plan to go full time? Do you have an office and staff? How committed are you?

Anytime you or your teammates have challenges in the business, all you have to do is apply the 7-point test. You will find the answer to the problems very quickly.

"Who's for real in your team?"

THE FEAR FACTOR

So many people let fear control them, hold them back, and slow them down.

When They Go Into Business, They Express So Many Fears

► Fear of what people will say

► Fear of rejection

► Fear of not knowing enough

► Fear of the competition

► Fear of failure

► Fear of speaking in public

► Fear of the uncertain

► And a lot more

"Fear is a luxury of your mind that you cannot afford."

Fear is not necessarily bad. Actually it can be a great asset. Remember all the good fears that you had?

Fear of losing that fired you up in sports competitions.

Fear of disappointing your parents that helped you excel in class and get good grades.

Fear of losing your job that keeps you working so hard.

Fear of ill health that motivates you to exercise and maintain a healthy diet.

Control Your Fear And Turn It Into Good Use

I used to fear all the negative things people might say, but then I realized that I would only prove them right if I listened to them.

I used to fear rejection. It killed me when people said No. But if I stopped, I feared I'd lose my next superstar because I know I'm only one recruit away from a big explosion.

I used to fear not knowing enough. I didn't want to be embarassed. But the fear of depending on other trainers and not being able to learn fast enough was more pressing.

> *"If I keep sitting in the passenger seat,*
> *I will never know the way."*

I used to fear the competition, but the fear of losing to them and missing the opportunity of a lifetime made me stronger everyday.

I used to fear speaking in front of crowds, but the fear of disappointing the team was even worse.

I used to fear failure, but the thought of going back to my job was even more depressing. That kept me going until I became successsful.

> *"I have so many fears in my life, but the biggest fear*
> *is being average and ordinary."*

We live with fear all our lives. Either we control fear, or fear will control us.

SUCCESS PRINCIPLES

YOU MUST:

1. HAVE A STRONG DESIRE

2. BELIEVE IN YOUR DESTINY

3. HAVE A STRONG REASON TO FIGHT FOR

4. HAVE A GOOD MISSION

5. HAVE A GOAL WITH A WRITTEN PLAN

6. HAVE A SYSTEM AND A MENTOR

7. HAVE THE ABILITY TO LEARN AND TO FOLLOW

8. HAVE COMPASSION FOR PEOPLE

9. HAVE FAMILY SUPPORT

10. STAY POSITIVE ALL THE TIME

"Change the way you think. Change your habit.
Change your life!"

THE FOUR KNOWS

"Know your enemy and know yourself.
You can fight a hundred battles and win
a hundred of them."

— SUN TZU

1. Know What You Want

▶ Know the reason you go into business. What difference can you make in your loved ones' lives? Your spouse's, your kids', your parents', and others'?

▶ Have a clear goal. How much money do you want to make? How soon will you be financially independent?

▶ Have a well-thought-out plan. How wide-deep-big do you want your team to be?

HAVE A SPECIFIC GOAL, AT A SPECIFIC TIME

Imagine if a travel agent asks you
where and when you want to travel,
and your answer is:
"Any destination is okay and any time
is fine with me."
It's your life. Be specific.

2. Knowledge

▶ Know the concepts, products, and services well.

▶ Understand and run the system.

▶ Recruit, build, and motivate.

▶ Know your people.

▶ Know your clients.

3. Know Yourself

▶ Do you have what it takes to win?

▶ Know your weaknesses—e.g., procrastination, shyness, fear of rejection—and conquer them.

▶ Know your strengths—e.g., positive attitude, mental toughness, perseverance—and take advantage of them.

▶ Know the price you have to pay, the sacrifices you're willing to make, in order for you to win.

4. Know That You're Going To Win

▶ If you don't, you might as well quit right now.

"It's your business to know."

30 DAYS RELENTLESS

"Never go home before 11 PM."

The day I totally changed my life… it didn't come the first month, and it didn't come the second month. About 5 to 6 months in the business, the day I was so sick and tired of being a loser, I made a mental decision that I would never go home every night before 11 p.m.

That was the toughest discipline call I made in my life. Every night, I was out in the field, whether I had appointments or not. I was out there, and I was not going home. That's why I drove around and around, and that's how I learned to drop by a prospect's or a team member's house. I would just stop by and talk business.

Night after night, I went out in the field. The first month was tough, but by the second month I was so busy because I had so many appointments. The first few weeks I had no appointments, but as I stopped by and dropped by enough people's homes, and as they gave me more leads and went out in the field with me, the activity I created snowballed and became unstoppable.

I just figured out that anyone who has a business is going to open their business every day. So I just did what a normal businessperson would do.

You're not for real until you can pass this test. When working for someone else, most of us have no problem going

> " *Can you be in business for 30 days straight? Can you stay out in the field until 11 PM? Can you be relentless and inevitable?* "

to work everyday. But when we go to work for ourselves, we can't do it. When we're in business for ourselves, when we're our own boss, when we can do anything we want, we end up doing nothing.

A large majority of people cannot go out in the field even once a week. A handful can barely go out a few days a week. Only a chosen few can be out there every day.

In our business many people who go out in the field for 4 hours every night end up making more money than people who work 8 hours every day at their job.

> I believe you can change your life in 30 days. You can change your habits in 30 days.
>
> If you're a late person, if you decide to be 10 minutes early to any appointment, job, or party for 30 days, you can be an early person for the rest of your life.
>
> If you can stick to physical exercise for 30 days without fail, you can have and keep that habit.
>
> If you go out in the field every night for 30 days, you will develop a winning habit that lasts a lifetime.

JUST DO IT

When your team does not move,

keep on moving yourself.

If your team does not recruit,

you recruit.

If your team does not sell,

you sell.

If your team does not go to the meetings,

you go to the meetings.

If your team does not go to the convention,

this is the reason for you to go.

You care for your team.

But you don't care.

You need them.

But you don't need them.

Just keep on keeping on.

A NEW DIMENSION IN TIME

"Time is a terrible thing to waste."

Before joining the business, my perspective of a day revolved around my J.O.B., which began at 8 in the morning and ended at 5 in the evening. Every day I woke up early to prepare for work, fought my way through traffic, and made sure to show up on time. When work was over at 5pm, I would pick up the kids from the babysitter, go home, take care of the kids, and watch TV while my wife fixed dinner. Then after dinner, we prepared lunch for tomorrow. We'd go to sleep early so that we could wake up early the next day.

But after joining the business and going out in the field in the evening, I realized that there are so many other people working, businesses operating, and services providing and making good money after 5pm. Restaurants, entertainment centers, financial services professionals, night shifters, etc.

As for myself, not too long in the business, I began to make more money after 5pm than before 5pm. My part-time income grew and surpassed my full time income. Ever since, I saw a new dimension in time. While most people were still trapped in their 8 to 5, I was out of it. I realized that when you limit your time working for a living, you hold your life back from your dream.

"There is no time limit for your dream."

THE KUNG FU MASTER

Once upon a time, high up in the mountains, there lived the greatest kung fu master of the time. Martial arts students all over the land came to learn from him. They worked hard, practiced day and night, and went through great sacrifices and pain. Many of them became famous and successful.

One day, a monk stopped by to visit him and asked, "Master, you produce so many successful disciples. Your reputation has spread all over. You should be very proud and happy, yet you seem to be sad and unsettled."

The master replied, "Sir, all my life, I trained thousands of students. I found most of them are good. The majority of them learn to be the fastest, strongest, and most powerful fighters. They come down the mountain to become generals, officials, and great martial artists. Some remember me and pay me a visit to offer gifts and thanks. They learned everything from me—except they don't want to do what I do. No one wants to come up here and replace me!"

TOO BUSY FOR YOUR DREAM

"You get busy all your life and then die."

The number one cause of failure in our business is lack of time.

"I don't have time," "I can't make it," "I have to work over-time," "I have a wedding to go to," "There's a party," "I have to pick up one of my relatives," "I'll be ready next month," "When I come back from the trip, I'll do it," et cetera, et cetera.

They show up to the office and disappear for a few weeks. They undergo licensing but can't finish. They want to go out to the field but can only do it once or twice. The minute they have some recruits, something always happens, and they can't work with them. Something always happens at the wrong time.

People are busy. They really are. I was one of them. Both my wife and I had full-time jobs. My job was quite demanding, so was my wife's. Between work, taking kids to school, pick-ing them up, preparing dinner, and doing household chores, we were a very busy couple.

But that was just the beginning. There was always something to do, somewhere to go. We drove our kids to school meet-ings, baseball practice, swimming lessons, piano lessons, and karate lessons during the week. And during the weekends, we'd have to prepare for a party, or go to somebody else's par-ty, or call someone to apologize for being unable to make it to their party. We went to birthday parties for kids, for adults, for friends, for in-laws. We celebrated baptisms, communions, weddings, anniversaries, graduations. We bought gifts for

Father's Day, Mother's Day, Valentine's Day, Christmas, New Year's. We barbequed for every playoff game, Super Bowl, and World Series.

Everybody invites everybody, and everybody is afraid to say No because we're afraid that when the time comes for us to throw a party, our kid's birthday, our BBQ, people won't have time for us. When we go to a party, we talk about the people who don't show up.

"It's a system whereby parties never stop!"

Then Monday morning comes. We go to work to pay our bills. Christmas arrives. One year passes by. Every year, the next year seems busier than the last. We turn 40, we turn 50, we turn 60, and then we're too old. Now we stay home alone because our kids and grandkids are too busy going to their parties, weddings, and barbeques.

With all this time on our hands, we get to watch TV. We turn on the Travel Channel to see all the wonderful places in the world that we weren't able to visit because we didn't have the time or the money.

Welcome to the busiest place in the world. I walked down this busy street half my life and finally woke up the day I saw the business presentation. I was fortunate because I was able to change. I didn't want to go through the rat race. I wanted my life back.

Unfortunately, most people are not that lucky. They can't wake up. They can't get out. They can't change. They have all the time in the world for their boss, their friends, their in-laws, and everybody else. But they never have time for their business. They're too busy for their own dreams.

Almost everybody has no time. A handful shows up sometimes. Fewer people work part-time. And of course, very few become full-time or go ballistic all the time.

> **WE HAVE 5 TYPES OF PEOPLE IN OUR BUSINESS:**
> 1. The No-timer
> 2. The Sometimer
> 3. The Part-timer
> 4. The Full-timer
> 5. The All-the-timer

You can never do anything in life if you don't have time.

You will definitely fail if you do things sometimes.

You make some money if you work part-time.

You make good money if you invest your full time.

But if you want to make a fortune, you must put your heart, your mind, and your effort into the business all the time.

"Either you follow other people's schedules or you follow your own schedule. Either you do it for you or you do it for others, but you certainly will be busy."

SOMETHING TO BELIEVE IN

So many people do things they don't really believe in. Millions of people wake up in the morning, commute to work, and show up at a job they don't really believe in. They don't see their future there. They report to a manager they don't really believe in either. They're not sure their boss takes the best interests of them and their family to heart. They go to lunch with their coworkers and have some casual conversations. They go home and watch TV while life passes them by. They love their family and their children, but they're uncertain whether the children will be successful because they're not successful.

For me personally, I came to a point in my life where I found that I had to make a decision. I went through that routine—the job, the situation with my family—and I told myself, if there's something I should do right now, I have to find something that I totally believe in and put my life into it. And the reason I am here is because I absolutely believe in what I do.

FAMILY BUSINESS

We cannot make a difference for families until we help our family first.

Over the years we found that having the family involved turned out to be the most incredible thing to happen to our family and to our lives. I don't think the work is the issue. But to be able to have the family help out in the business and help other people have brought us together.

I don't know about other families, but ever since I joined this business and I involved my family, I never had to explain what I do. When I travel long distance—and many days I'm not home—I tell my wife, when the kids ask where I am, you have two choices. You can say dad is going to work, or you can say dad is going out to do good things for our family and for other families. The first answer is a separation of family and business, the second makes business and family as one.

The bottom line is we do everything for ourselves and our family, and the main reason we are here is because we're doing something good for our family. Our mission is to make a difference for families. And this should be clear from the beginning.

Why is that so easy to understand when we go to work at a job? Our spouse supports it. Our children know it. What about this business? The family needs to give the same support here as with any job.

HELPING PEOPLE

*"To give pleasure to a single heart
by a single act is better than a thousand heads
bowing in prayer."*

— GANDHI

I grew up during the Vietnam War. I saw desperate situations everywhere. All the temples and the churches were packed with people, so were the refugee camps and military bases.

In our business, we pack our meetings and conventions with people. We talk about our crusade, our mission to help people. But how sincere are we about what we do?

There are so many people who say they want to help, but they hardly move. In fact, they can't even help themselves. They don't recruit, they don't go out in the field, they make no money, and yet they say they want to lead and impact others.

How desperate are people out there for an opportunity? How badly do they need help for their financial survival? Even still, there is so little action, so few appointments.

AGGRESSIVENESS

You are not aggressive enough:

If you sit in a meeting and you wish that more of your team should listen to this.

If you go to a convention and you sit in the back.

If you have a picture of your kids on your cell phone and your cash flow is down.

If you are in a meeting or on a conference call and you're not prepared to share.

If you failed a contest and you say that you will qualify the next time.

If you declare a goal you know that you can hit and you don't even do half of it.

If you ask your partner to go to a meeting and you both end up half an hour late.

If you have many appointments but you don't close any.

If you go back home because your appointment is cancelled tonight.

If you have no new names on your prospect list in the last 7 days.

If you have only one strong leg.

If you count on your team's production to pay your bills.

If you go home before 11 pm.

If you sit in front of the computer more than half an hour per day.

If you walk into a meeting and you don't know who on your team is in there and who is not.

If you come to a meeting later than your team and leave before them.

In a team meeting, you want to talk but you hold off because you think you are a small fish.

If you are on a conference call and you report zero results two weeks in a row.

If you don't have at least 2 personal recruits per month.

If your spouse asks you why the business is going south, and you say, "I don't know".

If your parents worry about you and tell you to find a job, you're not aggressive enough! You're not trying hard enough! You're not big enough! And you're not providing enough!

"A good ship is not built to stay
in the safe harbor.
It is built to sail to the thrill
of the yearning sea."

THE OFFICE TRAP

*"Many MDs open an office and keep it closed
most of the time."*

1. AN OFFICE DEMONSTRATES STRONG COMMITMENT.
You are not for real until you have your own office. Having
your own office shows that you take the business seriously,
that you are a true entrepreneur. You need an office to con-
duct interviews, do presentations, hold team meetings, etc.
By having an office, you move to the next level. Your team
will rise up because you are committed.

**2. YOU SHOULD HAVE AN OFFICE STAFF OR
SECRETARY TO HELP YOU WITH PAPERWORK.** It's hard
to tell people that you have a big business, yet you cannot
even afford an office and staff. Your staff should free you from
excessive paperwork, so you can focus on the main things.

3. YOU MUST GO TO WORK EVERYDAY. You must show
up at your office just like with any other business. This does
not mean that you lock yourself in that room and do not go
out to the field. But you should return to your office between
field work.

4. YOUR OFFICE IS A NEW OUTLET. If you want to have
lots of outlets in multiple locations, you must start one first.

But Avoid The Office Trap

▶ The minute they have an office, many MDs preoccupy
themselves with paperwork, PowerPoint presentations,
electronic upgrades, administrative procedures, etc. Instead
of becoming a builder, they become office managers or,

worse, secretaries. They spend more time in the office and less time in the field. They get comfortable conducting recruiting and sales presentations in the office. Field training suffers. Duplication slows down.

▶ On the other hand, some MDs have offices but keep it closed most of the time. They don't show up to work or don't show up at the office often enough. They're unpredictable. Their team is not so sure where they are. Imagine you go to the doctor's office, but the doctor is not in and has no set hours. This will hurt their business more than help.

▶ Your office should not be a financial trap. Don't open an office or a big office if you can't afford it. The financial pressure will affect your attitude and performance. Make sure you have consistent cash flow and ample reserves for business expenses.

▶ Don't let the office trap you from expansion. After opening their first office, many builders do not build other places. They're less mobile and tend to expect their team to come to them.

"Remember: Opening an office is an aggressive move to grow and expand your business—not the cause to trap you in and slow you down."

THE SIX-FIGURE TRAPS

"The invisible limitations."

It's doesn't matter what they said when they started. It doesn't matter what goals they declared the year before. It doesn't matter how much they said they love the team. It doesn't matter how much they said they want to help people.

What they said in the past carries no weight. It's their actions now that speak the loudest.

As soon as a six-figure income is achieved, most people, intentionally or unintentionally, slow down mentally first and physically after.

▶ When they hit 100K, a large majority of newly promoted MDs get trapped. They're too busy working in their business, opening their own office, and maintaining the base.

> ## Builder's Note:
>
> *"There are strange farmers in a strange land who grow a farm in the first few years but neglect it after that and expect it continue to grow and bear good crops forever."*
>
> **Most of these people don't realize that once they slow down, their 100K, 250K, or 500K income is not going to maintain either.**

▶ When they hit 250K, some pass the first level, building a few more MDs and expanding to a few more locations.

▶ When they hit 500K, very few move on. Very few keep building and expanding. They build good superbases, and the hierarchy starts growing. But they become distracted. They look for a new house and new cars. They no longer go out in the field. They'd rather motivate other people to do that. Their spouse no longer engages in the business like before. After all, it's their chance to enjoy the fruits of their labor.

Sometimes I wonder whether someone will move on to seven figures?

> *"Success has ruined many a man."*
> — BEN FRANKLIN

WHAT DO YOU MAKE?

1. Make a living
2. Make good money
3. Make a fortune
4. Make a difference
5. Make history

"At what level will you stop or slow down?"

MOST PEOPLE WON'T STAY

"If you're not so sure whether you will stay or not, why expect your people to stay?"

Quitting is one of the main characteristics of our business. Don't be so surprised! In fact, I'd be surprised if you are surprised.

In our business, people won't stay. They think they have nothing to lose when quitting. If they go to work, they can't quit. They have to pay the bills. If they spend a few hundred thousand dollars to buy a business, they won't quit either. They have loans to pay off. The bottom line is, most people only stick with a job or a business because they have no other choice.

"Most people think that they have nothing to lose when quitting, but what they don't know is that they lose a lot."

I remember every semester when I went to night school for adult continuing education. The classes were packed at the beginning of the semester. It was even difficult to find a parking space. But after 1 or 2 months, the classes were half empty. And by the end of the semester, I'd drive into a deserted parking lot. Every 6 months, the same thing repeats.

On the other hand, the college never had this quitting problem with daytime students.

Quit Within The First 72 Hours

Within the first 3 days, a new recruit talks to 10 to 20 of their friends and relatives. Guess what they're going to hear? Every negative criticism in the world. Most can't survive the first round of attack.

Quit Within The First 30 Days

These people are a little stronger than the first group. They do PPL, BMP, and invite. But people say No to them, jack them around, and stand them up. They might recruit one or two people. But unfortunately their recruit quits, so they quit too.

Quit Within The First Year

A handful stay. They recruit some people, get licensed, and begin to go out in the field. They make a few sales once in a while and go to meetings and conventions occasionally. They like the business but find it too tough. Many people don't buy from them. Their team is not committed. Their spouses don't give them support. Little by little, it will kill them.

You're Not For Real Until You Last More Than 18 Months

As with any new venture, the initial phase is very tough. Whether you open a restaurant, start a real estate agency, become a freelance artist, or launch a financial services career, the first 1 to 2 years are survival time, even if you try hard.

But if you hang on for the first 18 months, you may survive and have a long term commitment for the business.

There is no miracle here. This is not a get-rich-quick scheme.

You must want it bad. You must work hard. You must give your business total commitment.

"What about your job? Does it get you anywhere in the first 18 months?"

It Takes At Least 5 Years To Build A Good Business
My First 2 Years: Survival

▶ Prospected, invited a lot; few came

▶ Recruited some but they didn't last; didn't listen, didn't go to the meeting, didn't get licensed, didn't sell if they got licensed

▶ Learned to drop by, recruit, sell, and earn some money

"The best thing I learned was not to get killed by all the bullets that are shot at me everyday."

My Next 2 Years: Work, Work, Work

▶ Became full time

▶ Became a good producer and a good trainer

▶ Built discipline and winning habits

▶ Earned a six-figure income

▶ Learned to follow the system

▶ Began to have a vision

▶ Developed a strong passion for the mission

▶ Started building the base

My 5th Year: Became A System Builder

▶ Built a strong baseshop

▶ Built a strong foundation for a big hierarchy

▶ Understood the system and the business

▶ Built long distance

▶ Organized meetings and big events

▶ Became confident about my recruiting mentality, builder's mindset, meeting mentality, and leading by example

▶ Developed winning habits

▶ Became a major earner

▶ Stayed on track to my dream

"Yes, you can do it if you stay!"

JUST WANT TO BE ME

"About 26 years ago,
I no longer wanted to be a good husband.
I just wanted to be me."

I grew up in a poor family. My dad died when I was 16. My mother never worked outside of the home. My brothers and I had to work at an early age to support our large family.

I always wanted to be a good kid. I went to work and school at the same time. Every penny I earned, I gave to my mother, so she could have money to pay for expenses. Not only did I work hard at work, I worked hard to excel in school, so that my mom would be proud of me. Even after I got married, whatever money I could save I would send to my mom.

There were many times when I wanted to do things for myself—buy something, travel somewhere… but I set it aside, hoping that one day I would be able to do it. I constantly felt ashamed that I couldn't do more for my family. I looked at others who were richer than me, who were able to do more for their families than me. That killed me inside.

I always wanted to be a good husband. After I got married, I wanted to do so much for my wife. But I was a poor social worker. My income was limited. I also lacked many skills of a typical husband. Looking at people around me, not only could they afford nice

 things for their wives, they also knew how to fix the car, tend to the garden, build the deck, and hook up the computer. As for me, I'm terrible at those things. Everything I touched, I messed up. The more I tried to be a good husband, the more frustrated I became.

I was in a losing game.

I always wanted to be a good father. Then I had children. Whenever I read books on how to be a good father, I felt so small. I looked at all the good fathers on TV shows, and I felt ashamed. I couldn't afford things for my kids. I wasn't good at teaching them sports. I spent my time doing birthday parties and driving my kids around, but I wished I could be a better father.

I always wanted to be a good son-in-law. I wanted my wife's family to be proud of me. So no matter how busy I was, I would set aside time to do good things for my in-laws.

I always wanted to be a good friend, a good employee, and a good relative. I wanted to make people happy and feel good about me. Although there were times when I had financial challenges, as well as life challenges, I always put those people ahead of me.

When I reached the age of 36, I was a miserable man. I was poor. My job was insecure. My future was bleak. I spent all my life trying to make people happy, but I myself was unhappy. I did not feel good about myself.

Then, one Saturday morning, I saw the BPM. That changed my life entirely. I was so excited about the business opportunity. But I didn't know what to do between a full-time job, a family, a brand new business opportunity, and making everyone else happy.

I made a tough decision. I no longer wanted to be a good husband, a good father, a good son, a good son-in-law, or a good friend.

I just wanted to be me. I decided to stop making others happy and finally decided I just wanted to do things that made me happy.

I closed my eyes, plugged my ears, and moved forward, going after my dream. I did not fulfill much of my role as a husband. I let my wife take care of the children. I stopped hanging around my friends. Negativity spread all over. People told me I was crazy. They told me I was too much into money. They said that I wouldn't last too long.

But I endured, I made money, and I won. It was a long, tough fight, but it changed my life forever. After the first year in the business, I doubled my income. After the second year, I tripled it. By the third year, I made a six-figure income and retired my wife. I kept building a big team and a successful business. I became financially independent.

I found out an important thing. Before, I spent my life trying to make other people happy, but I was broke and unhappy. In reality, though, I wasn't able to help anybody, and they weren't so happy either.

Now, I spend my life for me. I live my dream every day. I am truly happy. But even better, I can also make my family's dreams come true. My wife doesn't need to go to work, and I am able to provide for my children and help people around me.

When I travel, I hear the flight attendant say, "Put on your oxygen mask first, before you help your children or others." I agree with that advice.

> *"It's hard to help others*
> *when you're unable to help yourself.*
> *It's hard to make others happy*
> *when you're unhappy."*

HANDWRITTEN SIGN FOUND ON THE WALL OF MOTHER TERESA'S ROOM

▶ *People are often unreasonable, illogical, and self-centered; forgive them anyway.*

▶ *If you are kind, people may accuse you of selfish, ulterior motives; be kind anyway.*

▶ *If you are successful, you will win some false friends, and some true enemies; be successful anyway.*

▶ *If you are honest and frank, people may cheat you; be honest and frank anyway.*

▶ *What you spend years building, someone could destroy overnight; build anyway.*

▶ *If you find serenity and happiness, others may be jealous; be happy anyway.*

▶ *The good you do today, people will forget tomorrow; do good anyway.*

▶ *Give the world the best you have, and it may never be enough; give your best anyway.*

▶ *For you see, in the final analysis, it is between you and God. It was never between you and them anyway.*

MY STORY

I grew up in a large and poor family during the Vietnam War. When my father, a failed businessman, died young, our family situation went from bad to worse. I was 16 at the time. My mother was in a state of desperation. She had never worked outside the home, so my brothers and I had to go to work to support the family. By some miracle, juggling between work and school, I was able to finish college, the only one in my family.

I was also the only one able to escape to the US when the war ended in 1975. At the refugee camp, I met Hoa, my friend in college. One year later, we married in Hawaii, and in 1978 we moved to San Jose, California. In the land of opportunity I found it hard to make a living. I worked many odd jobs before winding up in a social worker position, helping newly arrived refugees and immigrants resettle in America. I did the job well and quickly became the director of the agency.

Hoa worked as an accountant. We started a family and bought a small house. Our income was limited, and I had the additional burden of taking care of my family back in Vietnam where they faced incredible economic hardship.

By the time I was 36 years old, money was a real problem. Even though I was never a big spender, I was in debt and constantly worried about the future. My wife, on the other hand, grew up in a wealthy family and was always cheery and happy. Although we tried some business ventures, things never worked out.

Then one day in May 1985, while in the hallway of my office building, I bumped into a RVP (similar to a MD) from A.L.

Williams. She introduced herself and invited me to come to a BPM. That Saturday morning totally changed my life.

Walking out of the meeting, I felt like I was in heaven. I sat in my car and flipped through the information packet in awe of the opportunity. I heard angels sing. My prayers had been answered.

Excited, I raced home to tell Hoa. When I got home and relayed the good news, my friend who was visiting started laughing. He told me that I was the last person in town to learn about this deal. The rest of the weekend was depressing. Everybody I talked to told me that I made a mistake, that this scheme won't work, that I was just wasting my time.

Luckily, my return appointment was on the following Monday. At the second interview, all my doubts were resolved. I joined the business and owned the product the next day. I believed in the concept of protection and investing for the future.

That evening I took my RVP out in the field to see my brother-in-law and two of my best friends. I was quite hopeful, but nothing happened. After 8 appointments, all we got were Nos. It was one of the biggest shocks in my life. How could it be? After seeing the presentation, I joined and owned the product right away. Why are these people so difficult? Was I just too naïve? I wanted to quit, but I didn't. Somehow I knew that it wasn't me who made a mistake, it wasn't me who was wrong. So I continued on. It took me almost 3 weeks to have my first recruit, a cousin-in-law who ended up doing nothing.

I continued to struggle during the first months. I recruited a few people, but most did not stay for long. I got my license and made some sales but had trouble making money. For me, the business was an emotional roller coaster. I got pumped up going to the meeting but then became depressed the next day. I asked Hoa to join me for the meeting, but seeing me so miserable, she wasn't too thrilled about the business.

One night, about 4 months in the business, we attended a party with one of my best friends. He was a manager at a large tech company. I waited for this moment for quite some time. After other guests went home, I started to talk to the couple about the business. In the middle of the presentation, my wife mentioned that I did not make any money yet. Instead of continuing the recruiting presentation, that evening Hoa and I got into a fight about the business.

I was furious but realized the next day that Hoa was right. I was going to the meeting, I was constantly dreaming, but I was never fully engaged. That day was a turning point in my career. It was then that I decided to make money and never go home before 11pm.

The next 30 days were so difficult. I wandered around every night, prospecting, stopping by, and dropping by. A lot of people didn't want to see me. A lot of people who saw me said No or they want to think about it. Nonetheless, I continued to move on and did not go home until 11 o'clock.

Then things started to happen. I began to make some money. Within a few months, I was able to make as much money as my full-time job. I knew I needed my wife's support if I want to do it big. So by the time I saved $7,000, I took Hoa on a dream vacation to Paris. It was our first time in Europe.

My second year in the business my cash flow grew to more than double my full-time income. I was able to clean up all my debt and started saving seriously. Although I was doing well financially, I still felt miserable with the business. I recruited a lot of people, but they quit as fast as they joined. Very few stuck around, and those who stayed were not committed. Nobody seemed to want it bad. Personally, I was consistent and competed with local leaders to stay motivated. I had activities every day and developed a habit of having a goal and hitting my goal every month.

But I faced many challenges doing the business. Every time I was on stage, I had big fears. One Super Saturday I was asked to give a 5-minute talk. I didn't last more than 60 seconds. I also remember one BMP appointment I had in Sunnyvale. An engineer was helping his son with homework when I dropped by. He tried to listen to me for a while before losing patience. He looked at me and said, "I don't think I can do this every night like you. My kids are too important to me!" His words shook me to the ground. I was deeply hurt. What am I doing here? I asked myself. Why I am not staying home taking care of my kids? Is he a good father and a good husband while I am not? I sat in the car pondering this for a moment. Yes, I realized, he is a good father. He really cares for his kid. But I'm a good father also. I too care for my children's future. The difference is that while he cares for his kids at home, I fight for my family out in the field, just like my dad did when I was young. That realization was a major breakthrough for me.

I decided to run for the RVP position shortly after. I couldn't wait any longer. Most of my team had quit, so I had to pull through mostly with my personal effort. The summer of 1987 I made the leap to do the business full time. I always wanted to have Hoa stay home to take care of the children. I promised her that if we had our third child, she would stay at home. Our biggest challenge was timing. We had just quit both of our full-time jobs, and Alicia, our third child, was just born. Whereas before we had 3 incomes, the part-time business was now the only source of income for our family.

There was no turning back. Scared, I worked relentlessly, running nonstop, and survived. By the end of the year, I hit a six-figure income. Although no serious leader emerged, I was still hopeful. It took me another year until things started to grow. It was 1988. I became a good trainer, learned to over-lap leadership, and built wide and deep. My baseshop started growing. We had a good team. We learned to start early in the month and to finish strong. I promoted my first MD and soon after he went full time. We became one of the top 10 RVPs in the company that year and qualified for our first company trip to Europe. This time we went with class. Talk about seeing light at the end of the tunnel.

The next year we wanted to help our upline run for NSD (similar to CEO MD). We did our job and produced great results, qualifying for my family's first Hawaii trip. The second day in Hawaii, I was on the beach talking to one of the top leaders in the company about our recent success. He pointed out that with our big numbers, if we could just pump it up a notch, I could pre-qualify for NSD myself before the end of the month. He asked me if I could do it, and I told him I could.

That night I couldn't sleep. I kept thinking about the team at home. My body was in Hawaii but my head was in San Jose. Knowing that she could not keep me, Hoa let me fly home in the middle of our vacation.

I felt bad for Hoa and the kids. But being a NSD was what I had been dreaming about the past 4 years. I didn't want to miss my chance.

When the team saw me back at the office, they were shocked but understood my determination. We rallied and worked hard, monitoring and motivating each other every day until we made it to NSD. The real benefit of the run was that for the first time, we truly understood what it meant to make a vertical move. We understood the power of teamwork, commitment, and fighting to win. That year we rose to be among the top 10 NSD teams in the company. And the following year we built more leaders and qualified for the highest position, SNSD. We also made an effort to build long distance. Although we failed in Texas, we began to make headway in Southern California.

As we tried to make a difference for families, helping people at the kitchen table every night, the industry, the economy and America were all changing. An investment revolution was taking place. Laws and regulations changed. Products became more competitive. There was more competition and more challenges to our concepts and beliefs.

By the end of 1991, we decided to be part of World Marketing Alliance, opening a new chapter in our careers. Despite high expectations, we faced incredible setbacks for a new start up. In addition, most of our team lacked the experience, know how, and licenses to sell the new product.

Very few sales were made. People faced severe financial challenges. We saw a large number of people quit in 1992, and by the Spring of 1993 we called the team together to rally in Valencia, California. Only about 100 members were still with us. It was the worst of our careers but also the beginning of a great build up.

Despite the challenges, we focused relentlessly on recruits and built up our MDs. We began expanding in Texas, Florida, and the East Coast. By 1995, we had 2 CEO MDs. Our people made money and started to enjoy it. That's when the growth machine lost altitude. Our numbers dropped to half within a short period of time. Many of us mistook the beginning as the end.

To fix the problem, we knew we had to systematize the team, build a new generation of builders, and start a big movement of people. We organized a series of Train the Trainers throughout the country and built wider legs. That year we made a strong climb, and I surpassed a 7-figure income. In January 1997, we introduced the CEO Club building system to more than 3,500 team members at the San Francisco Marriott. It was an instant hit. By the summer of that year, we made a record 5000+ recruits and 22 million production in one month. We also made a record number of promotions. By January 1998, we had over 9,000 teammates at our New Year's convention in the San Jose Arena. We had the best builders, the best baseshops, the best superbases, and the best superteam builders. We were excited and felt invincible. Talk about great momentum.

Everyone grew and made money. Recruiting was easy. Building was easy. Selling was also easy. After all, the Dow kept climbing, and our clients were also very happy. Who could deny us success?

Most of us were quite optimistic and thought our success would last forever. Many people started to enjoy the fruits of their labor. They drove fancy cars, bought big houses, and leased beautiful offices.

Although recruiting slowed down, production was still good. And as the Dow kept climbing, people kept buying. Making money was not difficult.

But when the dot.com bubble burst in 2000, all of a sudden, the sky fell. By the end of that year, virtually no baseshop builders hit double-digit recruiting, and very few new builders were produced. After our biggest growth, we had our greatest decline.

Throughout 16 years of highs and lows, I learned that we cannot rely solely on a hot product or good market conditions. What we needed was a solid system. The system had to be a discipline to the new recruit from the day they join, not something they learn along the way. It had to be simple, clear and easy, so it can be duplicatable, because without duplication, there will be no long-lasting building. Most important of all, it had to be fast. It must solve the fast start problem in order to retain people.

Thus, in 2001 we introduced The System Flow. The System Flow helps us gather a large number of people, build them up, help them become a MD, and duplicate more MDs. We've been running The System Flow for over a decade now. We've worked on it and improved it, and tested it in Canada and Asia. And we continue to simplify the system, as simplification facilitates systematization. To further help our team build through the system, we wrote *The System Builder* book in the summer of 2002. In it, we break down the understanding of the building unit, the MD Club, and lay out a blueprint to build a MD Factory.

We are truly building a new distribution system that will change the industry and contribute to the people around us. The build up of the greatest generation of system builders has already begun. I believe the future builder will be much bigger than many builders in the past, and that's the way it should be.

— XUAN NGUYEN